05/22 t 3

Serena Gray is the author of T
Her work has appeared in C
Woman's Own

Also by Serena Gray

THE SLAG'S ALMANAC

BEACHED ON THE SHORES OF LOVE

Serena Gray

Futura

A Futura Book

Copyright © 1989 by Serena Gray

First published in Great Britain in 1989 by
Futura Publications, a Division of
Macdonald & Co (Publishers) Ltd,
London & Sydney

ISBN 0 7088 4322 0

Photoset in North Wales by
Derek Doyle & Associates, Mold, Clwyd
Printed and bound in Great Britain by
BPCC Hazell Books Ltd
Member of BPCC Ltd
Aylesbury, Bucks, England

Futura Publications
A Division of
Macdonald & Co (Publishers) Ltd
66-73 Shoe Lane
London EC4P 4AB

A member of Maxwell Pergamon Publishing Corporation plc

Contents

PART I

Surviving The Male Drought and Related Matters

1

Terrorism and You

One night recently, I was sitting on the patio, working on my tapestry depicting the history of the Women's Movement over the last 100 years, when I found myself thinking about the strange way in which things come around. Miniskirts came back into fashion, red lipstick came back into fashion, fifties music came back into fashion, paisley came back into fashion, fishnet stockings (despite everything my mother said) came back into fashion – and now, against all odds, men are back in vogue.

In the fifties every girl's dream was to grow up with few enough physical defects to be able to fall in love and get married and live happily ever after. By the end of the sixties, however, the sexual revolution was blazing through even the usually stable suburbs of the Western world, and many people were convinced that marriage was dead (and many more, most of them women, were willing to kill it if it wasn't). Over the seventies the fight for female equality was carried out in the boardrooms and bedrooms of this weary old planet, as women campaigned for maternity leave and day care centres and equal pay and opportunity and the right to abortion and the right to have someone else change the baby's nappies or cook the supper or stay up till three in the morning sewing up the angel costume for the Christmas play. Singles bars were thriving and women were embarking upon successful careers and full and independent lives, dating men the way men had always dated women, without guilt or apology and with a full diary and more than one basket for the depositing of eggs (or, as my friend Sue puts it, having our cock and eating it too).

And then came the eighties. The decade of Ronald Reagan, Margaret Thatcher, the Falklands War, Chernobyl, yuppies, capitalism defended by the Holy Bible, Black Monday and the famous *Newsweek* headline of June 2, 1986: 'The Marriage Crunch'. It was in that article that the women of the First World were told in no uncertain terms what many of them had already begun to suspect. Eligible men (meaning, one assumes, men who are vaguely sane and faintly solvent, and not so young that you'd have to teach them which fork to use for the fried goat's cheese starter nor so old that the chances of them dying in their sleep are greater than the chances that they'll be able to get it up in the first place) were becoming, like the white whale, bloody hard to find.

According to 'The Marriage Crunch', a college-educated woman, single in 1986, at the age of thirty has only a twenty percent chance of ever marrying. By the age of thirty-five this same woman had better have a very good vibrator, be a mean hand with your basic household tools, and have a lot of hobbies, because her odds of finding a man to live with her have dropped to five percent. By the time she is forty, no matter how successful, or talented, or intelligent, or beautiful, or kind, or personable she might be, no matter if she can whip up a six-course gourmet meal after a ten-hour day prosecuting organized crime, no matter if she has just won the Nobel Peace Prize or the Pulitzer Prize for journalism, no matter if she is one of the most

IN THE 50s A GIRL'S DREAM WAS TO GROW UP
GET MARRIED AND LIVE HAPPILY EVER
AFTER, BUT THEN CAME THE SEXUAL
REVOLUTION AND A GIRL'S DREAM TODAY
IS TO GROW UP, GET MARRIED AND LIVE
HAPPILY EVER
AFTER.

important artists, politicians, or tango dancers of the
twentieth century, no matter if she spends all her free
time shopping for the bedridden or rowing out on the
ocean in a tiny inflatable to save the whales: by the
time she is forty this same woman has more chance of
being murdered by a terrorist than she has of finding a
husband.

It is important to mention here that this problem is
not one that is confined solely to women who have
squandered their youths becoming well-rounded
people, women so old (thirty or forty or, God forbid,
fifty) that no one would expect anyone to want them
anyway. For although the statistics show that while
'younger' women operate in a market where supply
and demand are reasonably balanced, once into the
twenties people of the female persuasion begin to find

that things look a little bleak. Once a girl is out of her teens or out of school, the Saturday night date goes the way of the dodo. Once the group you used to hang out with has broken up and all your friends are paired off and spending their spare time doing the sorts of things that couples do (entertaining other couples and trudging around the garden centre together on weekends with small fir trees and large rubber plants in their arms), and your own days are taken up with work (assuming, of course, that the work you do isn't managing Manchester United or the Chicago Bears), the only men you tend to meet are either married, or not married for a good reason.

And so, *naturellement*, men are back in demand. Suddenly, having a man, like having a miniskirt, has become important again. Where ten or twenty years ago the books written for women were all about asserting ourselves and understanding the ways in which men had historically manipulated and taken advantage of us, about being independent and enjoying our freedom and our rights as human beings, about finding ourselves and not turning into Barbie Dolls, now they are all about finding HIM – and having found him, understanding him, keeping him happy, and keeping him, come hell or high water. Where ten or twenty years ago women were dressing in sensible clothes and practical shoes (having broken that last high heel over his head when he suggested that her opinion on *ciné vérité* wasn't worth having), repair manual gripped under the arm and a sureness in the step, decking any man who dared to hold a door open or pull back a chair, now those same women have stilettos, tortured hair-dos and tight skirts that make running from muggers difficult, and sing 'I Enjoy Being a Girl'.

What it all boils down to is that never before in the history of this planet have there been so many stupendously eligible women (women with good jobs and their own flats and full diaries; women with good credit ratings and enviable record collections and cars that their fathers didn't hand down to them), and so few equally eligible (or even available) men.

There are hundreds of personal columns; scores of computer dating clubs; thousands of books telling you what's wrong with men, what's right with men, what's wrong with you, how to handle men, how to make love to them (assuming, that is, that you're ever likely to get that close), how to get them to marry you; millions of magazine articles telling you how to improve your hair and your ankles, your skin and your posture, your patience and your pesto; and an intricate and sophisticated network of mothers all over the globe doing their damnedest to bring their children together. But despite all of this the last time you went out with a man was either a blind date (your best friend's cousin, who finds his job of teaching English to Japanese bankers both stimulating and worthy of hours of conversation, was visiting and she blackmailed you into going out with them), or by mistake (he thought you were someone else).

'So,' you say, 'what's a person to do? Every friend I have has invited me to dinner to "meet someone" and nothing has come of it. I've been through the lot: divorced journalists with drinking problems, ex-SAS men with communication problems, shy accountants who cry whenever they hear Judy Garland sing 'Somewhere Over the Rainbow', balding merchant bankers who unwind by doing T'ai Chi. How many meals of spaghetti bolognese and how many glasses of cheap wine am I expected to take?'

'So what?' you say. 'I never wanted a long-term, live-in relationship. I've no intention of swapping my Gucci for a nappy bag. I've got a one-hole toothbrush holder and that's the way it's going to stay. Like the camel, you can consider me the ship of the desert.'

'Don't make me laugh,' you say. 'I made up my

mind a long time ago that if I can't have Bruce Springsteen I don't want anyone. Boyfriends are like chickenpox – something you have once and don't want to have again.'

These are difficult times, to be sure. For those of us who believe that the sexual revolution is as dead as Rin Tin Tin and that women have finally returned to their senses and are once more interested in the right things (in finding a partner who will give them security, children, a nice home, a Suzuki jeep, and – hopefully – no sexually transmitted diseases), it is clear that something will have to be done. She who waits for her prince to come (the joke used to go) won't have long to wait. But she who waits for her prince to turn up (the warning now goes) will find that he got distracted on the way and is married to someone else and living in the suburbs.

And even those of us who enjoy our solitude and independence – those of us who think that getting a Valentine's card only from our parents and our best friend is more than compensated for by the fact that if you leave the stereo on all night by mistake no one's going to wake you up in the morning shouting about dust and micro-chips and electric bills – would admit that men do have their uses. Most of us wouldn't mind a little romance now and again. Candlelit dinners for one do nothing more than save electricity. You can take men dancing. It's nice to have someone to watch *It Happened One Night* on the video with. You can't eat a whole pizza by yourself, and if you put it in the freezer it always breaks out of the foil you've wrapped it in and the mushrooms and peppers fall off. If you have a boyfriend your mother will stop asking you why you don't have a boyfriend. If you have a boyfriend your friends won't feel that they can't invite you to dinner because you ruin the numbers (or, alternatively, they won't feel that if they invite you to dinner they also have to invite brother Ted, the bachelor business-school lecturer, who though he does have a pulse has little else in common with the living). If you have a boyfriend you will have something to complain about when your friends are all moaning about their husbands and lovers. If you live with a man you will know why you're unhappy and not waste precious years of your life worrying that you're going through an early menopause when you're not.

2

IS THERE REALLY A PROBLEM?

There is really a problem. And unless you are under twenty, live on a military base, and look like Kelly McGillis, chances are you not only know this already, but you also know that it affects you.

Walk into any office, any hairdresser's salon, any trendy bar, any aerobics class, the local swimming pool on ladies' night – any place, in short, where women can be found together – and what you'll hear the single women talking about is the shortage of men. Women who used to meet every Monday night to raise each other's consciousness now sit around drinking gin and laughing hysterically any time someone plays Tammy Wynette singing 'Stand by Your Man'. The graffiti in the ladies' that used to say 'Who Needs Men?' now says 'Who Can Find One?' The waitress, overhearing you and your friend discussing the fact that the last man to lay a hand on you was taking blood, will pull up a chair and start telling you how she took up wrestling just so someone would put his arms around her.

'But my mother says there are men around,' you protest. Wise up. It was also your mother who told you you looked good in glasses and that, in time, you would grow. It was your mother who assured you that real men were more interested in character and personality than cup size or firm thighs. It was your mother who always maintained there was nothing wrong with your nose. Mothers – for all the best reasons – are paid to lie. It's in their contracts. And even when they aren't lying, it doesn't mean that they are telling the truth. Mothers use mother-speak. This means that rather than tell you the truth, your mother will tell you either: a. what you want to hear; b. what she wants to hear; c. something that both of you would like to hear; d. the literal as opposed to the real truth (e.g., your mother tells you that that shade of blue looks lovely with your colouring, which is true; what she doesn't tell you is that the way the jacket is cut makes you look as though you've stuffed oranges into your bra).

Of course there are men around. There is, for example, the boy at the supermarket checkout, the one who always picks up the bag of vegetables to be weighed from the wrong end. There is the unsmiling man who hands you stamps when you pay for your petrol (but only if you ask him first). There's the rather dishy man in the black Porsche who beeps his horn and shakes his fist at you because your Volkswagen inadvertently brushes his side-view mirror. There's the tetchy man whose underwear somehow gets mixed up with your coloured wash in the launderette. There's the fellow in the corner grocery who looks at your hips very much the way your mother would when he notices you putting that bag of chocolate digestives into your shopping basket. There are the husbands and brothers and lovers and boyfriends of relatives, acquaintances and friends. There are cops (never around when you want one) and lorry drivers (always around when you don't), dentists and builders, plumbers, exterminators and hairdressers, shoe salesmen and telephone repairman and riverboat captains.

There are men all over the place. But there's no one you would want to go and see *Poltergeist 3* with so you could land in his lap during the scary bits. There's no one whose saliva you might want to mingle with yours. No one to whom you could teach the secret delights of chocolate mousse at three in the morning.

For once, it seems, it is not your mother's fault.

What happened then? Have all the good men been abducted by sex-crazed women from another planet? Have they all moved to Okinawa? Have they all taken vows of silence and celibacy and retreated to some Tibetan monastery to await the end of the world (which, to give them credit, doesn't look as though it will be all that far off)? Were there, perhaps, never that many good men in the first place? Was it always simply a case of learning to like eating slugs because that was all that you were offered? Is this, perhaps, the male revenge for the feminist movement, the retribution for all the nights the guys had to spend on their own while their women went out with the girls from the office or worked late, leaving them with Sunday's leftovers and nothing good on television? Was my grandmother Sadie right when she prophesied in 1971 that no good would come from women wanting to be treated as human beings? (What Sadie actually said, waking up unexpectedly towards the end of a family Christmas dinner, was that homosexuals and feminists were asking for trouble. As the rest of the assembled gathering had been debating whether or not that year's pudding was better than the previous year's, Sadie's comment caused not a few moments of stunned silence.) Or is it simply, as my friend Eliza has been saying for the past few years, that all the good men are either married or otherwise engaged?

Part of the responsibility for this situation can be laid directly at the grubby feet of Life. Not only has the

custom of drowning girl babies at birth at least tempo-
rarily gone out of fashion, but Nature, knowing what
we would be up against, has made sure that girls are a
lot more durable and long-lasting than boys. She has
also made sure that we have a less egocentric and
broader world view than men, and that we are more
practical and mature in our tastes and desires.

What does this mean? That a man will eat crisps and a
cola for breakfast while a woman will first feed the
children and then have some porridge? More or less.

What it means is that if a man's ideal woman when he
was a callow and slightly silly boy of sixteen was the
Playboy centrefold for August, then his ideal woman
when he is fifty-eight, head of a billion-pound law firm,
a respected judge known for his intelligence and vision,
and a man who reads *Finnegan's Wake* for fun, will still
be that buxom beauty with the three-inch nipples as
pink as bubblegum and the Lolita pout who likes dogs
and walking in the rain and water skiing ('Topless, of
course. I just love to feel the spray on my body'). And
what that also means is that – cossetted and protected
by women all their lives, and brought up to believe that
when it comes to life forms everything else was just
practice – men have a longer shelf-life than women.

For the sad truth is that no matter how many times
your friends say to you, 'Old, you're not old. Look at
Cher', or 'Look at Tina Turner', or 'What about Joan
Collins? Isn't she a role model for us all?' the standards
by which a man is judged as a sexual object are not the
same ones used to judge a woman. A man can be as old,
as fat, as funny-looking, as boorish, as charmless, as
obnoxious as can be; he can have veins on his cheeks or
hair growing out of his nose or one eyebrow that crosses
his entire forehead; he can look like he's twelve months
pregnant or smell like low tide – and he will still find
someone to love him, still find someone to call him
honey and pick up his socks from the bathroom floor.

This is indeed a curious world. A bald, flabby,

grumpy man of sixty who is a mediocre lover, a terrible cook, and a shoddy housekeeper, a man who wears nylon shirts and looks his best on a dark night, would not think it in the least bit odd, or unusual, or just a little unjust from an evolutionary standpoint, to find himself dating a cute twenty-three-year-old who finds his jokes funny, his maturity sexy, his appalling taste in clothes and home furnishings masculine, and his domestic helplessness endearing. Whereas an attractive, intelligent woman of forty who does her own car repairs, has a fulfilling and interesting career, can cook like you always wished your mother had cooked, has a great sense of style, an infectious sense of humour, holds world championships in backgammon and break-dancing, and is studying for a Ph.D in oriental religions when she isn't reading to the blind, thinks she's died and gone to heaven if a man under twenty-five doesn't tell her she reminds him of his mother.

'Why is this?' you, rightly, want to know.

Very simply, this is because women look for different things in men (things like character, security, companionship, intelligence, responsibility, friendship, humour, guidance, stability – things that they may, of course, never find) than the qualities that men seek out in women (physical attractiveness, sexuality, adoration, maternal strength and loyalty, physical attractiveness). As Eliza said when her first husband ran away to Amsterdam with the *au pair*, 'If men could think as well as they can see the world wouldn't be in the mess it's in today.'

And so it is that somewhere in her early thirties a strange thing happens to a woman: too old to be considered a sexual object and too young to be given a seat on the bus, she becomes invisible. It doesn't matter how good she looks, how keen her mind, or how pure her heart. She might as well be made of glass. 'You see that woman over there?' you say to the men on the scaffolding. They occasionally break from their labour to shout

endearments to passing girls, so you know that their eyesight is unimpaired. Down the street comes a handsome, thirty-four-year-old woman wearing a bright red cape and carrying twenty-five silver balloons in the hand that isn't holding the chimpanzee. The men on the scaffolding follow your pointing finger. 'What woman?' they ask.

A man, however, suffers no such fate. As long as he isn't taped together and still has a heartbeat, a man can be desirable well into his sixties – and if he's rich, powerful, famous or overbearing enough, well into his seventies and eighties. 'Even if he's bossy and domineering and won't let you play your Patsy Cline records when he's in the house?'

Even if, in the middle of a serious argument, he is likely to lean over, pat your hand, and say, 'Honey, let's remember what time of month this is.'

A curious world and curiouser still. For the implications of the *Newsweek* article are nothing if not that the woman who spends her twenties becoming educated, self-reliant, and a success in her chosen career is wilfully missing out on her chance to find a husband. 'Poor old Ludmilla,' her friends all say. 'Can you imagine? She went to all the trouble of going to a good university, and instead of finding herself a doctor or a lawyer or a future small-arms manufacturer, she got three degrees, a high-powered and important job with an environmental pressure group and a special citation from the UN, and has nothing to look forward to now but staring down the barrel of an Uzi.' And a piece in *The Times*, following a 1988 survey, reported it as showing that 'many successful women in their mid-thirties lead solitary and emotionally unfulfilling lives'. Although the survey obviously made no attempt to measure just how emotionally fulfilling the lives of women who do not lead solitary lives might be, the implication once again is clear. You can have one, but you can't have both.

'Oh, what?' you say. 'Just a minute. How come a man can have a career and a family but a woman can't?'

Because men have wives, who support and encourage them and raise their families and are understanding about that little fling with the Greek travel agent, and women have husbands who expect them to behave like wives.

'But that's not fair!' you cry.

In a world where Ronald Reagan is made President and Nelson Mandela is put in prison, you want justice?

IS THERE A SOLUTION?

Opinions differ.

My friend Jane, who has been a sucker for self-improvement ever since she was nine and thought that if she tied her feet to the bed every night and got her sister to pull on her arms she would become taller, says that the solution lies with you yourself.

There are girls who sail through their teens like a boat with a good wind behind it in a calm sea (and with an auxiliary engine for times of trouble). These girls were never too tall, too short, too thin, or too plump. They were never awkward or gawky or spotty. They never had to refuse to leave the house in daylight. These girls never went through what your mother called 'the ugly duckling period'. ('But you just wait till you see what a beautiful swan you're going to be,' your mother would say with her kindest smile, mother-speaking her little heart out. 'Won't the boys look at you then?' 'But they look at me now, Mum,' you sobbed. 'Only instead of asking me for a date they call me Moby Dick or pretend to throw up.' 'Don't be ridiculous,' your mother would soothe. 'You teen-agers, you take everything so personally.')

These girls were never nudged, let alone plagued, by self-doubt. They didn't spend half their adolescence staring at themselves in anything that threw back a reflection – are my thighs too thick? are my breasts too small? if I curve my back will they look bigger? is one eye larger than the other? which one? if I suck in my cheeks will I look as though I have bone structure? is that a blemish? They didn't try every ointment, cream, lotion and treatment ever invented (by men) that promised to turn them overnight into the sort of girl who could advertise lipstick or instant soup or go out with a rock star (they didn't have to, of course: they already were that sort of girl). They didn't slavishly read every beauty and fashion magazine that came out, religiously doing the three-minute exercises for flatter tummies and straighter backs, bolting themselves into the bathroom with all the hot water taps running and a towel over their head to give themselves the Miracle Steam Treatment for Oily Skin and Blackheads, while outside their father banged on the door wanting to know if they'd died.

When they went to dances, these girls danced. Unlike the rest of us, who either huddled together at one end of the room trying not to look like unsold cattle or locked ourselves in the ladies', reading the book we brought with us because we knew this would happen or sobbing silently in the end cubicle because we knew this would happen.

On those long weekend nights when you and I went to the cinema with our best friends (equally unattractive and undesirable girls who either did a lot of horseriding or had pictures of pop stars taped to every wall of their room), these girls went out on dates with real boys, not the reject sons of someone their mother played Scrabble with. They went on dates, they got drunk, they got kissed, and they took their bras off in the backs of parked cars while the windows steamed up and their heads were banged against the door handles.

And all through those anguished years of teenage-hood, you clung to those inspirational words sung by Snow White in her clear, sweet voice, 'Someday my prince will come.' And all through those adolescent nights of the tear-soaked pillow, those nights when to hear Roy Orbison sing 'Only the Lonely' was to know that someone understood, you believed your mother when she said, 'It'll happen when the time is right. Don't worry, Mr Right will come along.' It made sense, didn't it? 'Ah, yes,' you told yourself, 'what faultless logic. Somewhere in this world is the man who is my perfect mate. A man created just for me. A man born to love me for ever and ever. A man who will find my toenail fetish doesn't disgust him. A man who likes short-waisted women who snore and go to bed with their hair wrapped around beer cans. A man who is fascinated by my knowledge of Early Etruscan art. I'll wait for him.'

And did he come?

Well, someone came. Someone who seemed like Mr Right, or, at the very least, Mr Maybe, for the first few hours, days, or years – only in the end he turned out to be Mr Big Mistake. How could I waste so much time on a man who hates Bruce Springsteen? you ask yourself later. How could I throw away the best years of my life on a man who thinks Bo Derek is misunderstood? On a man who always fell asleep when I was talking to him, and who never even noticed the butterfly tattoo on my inner left thigh? On someone who not only constantly reminded you that the art of conversation was dead, but who was probably the chap who killed it in the first place, you ask yourself later? On a bozo? A cold and heartless bastard who would have made Stalin look like a generous soul? Never mind, you comforted yourself, just because Mr Right is a little late doesn't mean he isn't coming at all. By the time he does arrive I'll really be ready for him. I'll be experienced and mature and read up on my *Kama Sutra*. I'll be swept into his arms and instantly forget about all the years I've spent going out to folk dance classes with my cousin Carla.

The clock ticks on. The stack of frozen dinner cartons under the sink mounts. Every time some strange man in the supermarket asks you which aisle the tinned soups are on your heart skips a beat: is this him? Could this man in the blue parka with the packet of rice cakes in his trolley be the one? Shop assistants start calling you madam; the first flush of youth is over. Once again thirty is beginning to seem a long way away. Where the hell is he? Has he been kidnapped by some fringe religious group or tragically killed in a motorcycle accident? Or is he simply living in comfort and contentment with a woman named Marlene, father of her children, walker of her dog, and installer of her bathroom tiles, unaware that he has married the wrong woman and is living a life that isn't his?

Waiting is out. Jane says that the girl who waits will find herself not woken by a kiss but buried alive. 'Finding a man is a serious business. If you wanted to buy a car, would you just sit around waiting for someone to park one with a For Sale sign in its rear window in front of your house?'

Well, no, I don't suppose I would, I fib.

'If you were a stockbroker, would you just stay in the kitchen all day, practising your chocolate soufflé and waiting for someone to call you with a hot tip?'

Come on, Jane, don't be silly.

'Serena, do you think Margaret Thatcher got where she is today by making the coffee at Party meetings and waiting to be asked for her opinion?'

That does seem unlikely.

'If you want something,' says Jane, 'you have to go out and get it. You have to be aggressive, not passive.

You have to take the initiative. If you want to find someone of your own to leave the toilet seat up all the time you will have to approach the problem in a scientific and businesslike manner. You will have to make plans and then carry them out.'

Um, correct me if I'm wrong, but doesn't this smack a little of the manipulation and ensnarement techniques of which women have historically been accused? Isn't this playing into the stereotype of the predatory female and the innocent male, listing to the side on which he wears the ball and chain?

'For heaven's sake, Serena,' says Jane. 'Don't tell me even you can be conned by that sort of propaganda? Do you think men don't have methods of seduction? Do you think politicians and businessmen and the barons of the art and entertainment industries are guileless? Do you think Barry Manilow became the idol of millions without a strategy?'

Nor is Jane the only one who will tell you that if you want to meet a man you will have to go out and find him. Your friends will tell you this. Your workmates will tell you this. Total strangers will tell you this.

'You should go out more,' says my mother. 'Meet people.'

'But I do meet people,' I defend. 'I've made at least five new and genuine friends in the last year.'

'Boys?'

'Girls.'

'—'

'And I went to that Women against War meeting last week. And I went to a signing at that feminist bookshop the week before. And Sally and Mary and I are going out to raise hell tomorrow night. And –'

'Not women,' interrupts my mother. 'People. You have to go where you'll meet some men. Take my advice.'

You do have to admit, of course, that – as risky as it is to take advice from a woman who once assured you that eating the crusts on your sandwiches would make your hair curly – it does make a weird kind of sense. If you were in the market for a slinky black number with gossamer shoulder straps would you hot-tail it to the army surplus store? Not on your life. So going where men are to find one is a perfectly reasonable theory. It is Jane's theory, and one she has put into practice at least three times a week for the past five years.

But, as with many perfectly reasonable theories (like democracy and socialism and free enterprise and putting in an extension phone yourself using the official kit with its clear instructions), out in the field things don't always go the way the strategists had planned.

The person who wants to find someone to go to restaurants with her so she'll be able to try the things on the menu that are for two will need courage.

The woman who would like to have someone tucked in beside her at night so that when the burglar does come through the bathroom window she can make her mate get up and do something about it will need fortitude.

The girl who is bored with being able to come and go as she pleases and longs for someone to nag her every time she stops for a drink after work or comes home later than she'd promised will need stamina.

She who is bored with a social life that consists of pleasant evenings and stimulating conversations with her varied and fascinating friends, and recalls with fond affection the years she spent with men whose idea of a dialogue was for her to ask, 'Would you like some coffee [tea, a drink, home-made ravioli, me to nip over to France for that brie you liked so much when you were there on holiday in 1981 ...], dear?', and for him to answer, 'Um, yes, but don't make it too strong like you usually do' should be prepared for the worst.

'The course of true love never did run smooth,' as Shakespeare, with his fine sense of understatement, once said. To which I can only add the immortal words, touched by the wisdom of her eighty-five years, that my grandmother Sadie said to me on the occasion of my first marriage. 'Well,' she said, brushing the hair out of my eyes, flicking a piece of fluff from my veil, 'I don't suppose you know what you're doing, but I wish you all the luck in the world.'

'That's very generous of you, Granny. Thank you very much.'

'Don't thank me,' said Sadie. 'You're going to need it.'

ATTITUDE, OR, IS IT TIME TO COMPROMISE?

You meet your mother for a Saturday of shopping and lunch in town, where stores are conveniently placed near one another and there are benches on which older women with bad feet and veins can stop for a rest without having to worry about being mowed down by hordes of crazed shoppers. She needs something to wear to the theatre the next time her group has a night out. You spend a couple of pleasant hours wandering into this shop and out of that one. You spend fifty-eight minutes of this time looking for a dress that isn't too short, too long, too bright, or too dark, that won't make her look like mutton dressed up as lamb but that also won't make her look like a little old lady. You don't shout at her in public (as you have once or twice been known to do in the past) because she makes you go into the changing room with her and hold her coat up as a screen. You don't lose your temper when she decides that she doesn't like the three dresses she brought into the changing room with her, and makes you go out for three more (which she doesn't like either); nor do you lose it later when, in another shop, she decides that she liked the first dress she tried on, which is exactly like the last dress she bought so she'd have something to wear when she went out to the theatre with her group. You do say, once or twice, 'Oh, Mum,' when she shouts across the sportswear department, 'Look at this, dear. Don't you think it would suit you? It wouldn't show up your hips.'

But you count it as a significant step in your efforts to build up a mature and adult relationship with your mother that she is willing to go to the kitchenware department with you in search of the perfect herb mill, and that it takes a full five minutes before her attention starts to wander and she tells you again how she once put some seasonings on your father's steak and he thought it must be off. 'Salt and pepper,' says your mother, 'was good enough for Cromwell and it's good enough for us.'

Throughout all of this, your mother-daughter conversation has been polite and superficial – what has happened recently in the life of her neighbour's dog, what the weather is doing to your hair, how your cousin Harriet is marrying the lawyer who did her divorce, why you have no luck with your roses – thus lulling you into what will turn out to be a totally false sense of security and well-being.

You tell your mother about your latest promotion, and she says, 'Oh, that's nice, dear.' You entertain her with your adventures in re-tiling the bathroom all by yourself, and she says, 'You must take after your father. I was never any good at that sort of thing. My hands are so delicate.' Other shoppers smile at you pleasantly as you trundle by, reassured by the sight of such a well-behaved mother and daughter that all is well with the nuclear family.

Then you stop for lunch.

You go into the basement restaurant of the largest store. It is inoffensively decorated in cheery colours and hanging plants, so that it looks, in fact, like any one of a million such establishments all over the planet, confirming our hopes that the Cold War is indeed over and we are truly becoming one world. You find a table in the corner, one with two extra chairs so your carrier-bags, raincoats, umbrellas, handbags, and the sweater your mother always carries, just in case, can all sit down as well. A tired-looking waitress whose thoughts are clearly not on you takes your order three times, confusion setting in because she can't seem to understand what 'salad without dressing' means, and because your mother can't make up her mind as to what she wants. The waitress brings you the drinks of two other people, then returns with yours, but forgets the water. You are trying to identify the music that is playing in the background (which, like something in a dream, is familiar but unfamiliar at the same time, as though 'F**k Like a Beast' is being played by Mantovani and His Orchestra) when your mother says brightly, 'So, darling, have you met any interesting men lately?'

You smile like the waitress. 'No,' you say, in a quiet, even voice. 'Did I tell you that Linda, Janet and I are going to paddle up the Amazon for our holiday this year? We thought we'd do something really different.'

'That's nice,' says your mother. 'Just when was the last time you had a date?'

You say, 'Mum …'

Your mother's voice gets just that tiny bit louder and more precise. 'I don't know why you always try to shut me out,' she complains. 'I'm your mother. I'm interested in you. I want to know what's happening in your life.'

Several people at nearby tables glance over. There is no doubt but that they are all themselves mothers, and each gives yours a sympathetic look.

'I'm not shutting you out,' you hiss back, knocking the little bowl of sugar envelopes on the floor as you lean forward. 'I told you about my job. I told you about my night course in advanced accountancy. I told you about my black belt in karate. I told you about the seminar my company wants me to teach in Miami next spring. I told you about the tune-up I gave the car. I asked for your opinion on the curtains I'm making for the living room. How am I shutting you out?'

'Pick up the sugar, dear,' says your mother. 'You can't just leave it on the floor. People will think you were brought up on the streets.'

You crouch beside the table and start retrieving the sugar.

'You shut me out,' your mother says to the top of your head, 'because you won't tell me about your personal life.'

You surface so fast that you drop the sugars. 'Did you want to hear about my last bout of cystitis?' you ask a little less sweetly than you'd intended. 'It was a real doozy.'

'That's not what I mean and you know it,' says your mother. 'Don't you think I have a right to know who you're seeing? Are you trying to hide something from me?'

You have turned your attention back to the floor, but even without looking up to read the expression on her face you know that she is remembering the two years you told her you were living with an air hostess named Lilah (who, therefore, was never in the country when your mother paid her visits), who turned out to be a heavy metal drummer named Luke.

'Mum,' you say gently, sitting once more in your chair, 'I'm not hiding anything. I have nothing to hide. There are no men in my life.'

'And just why is that?' your mother wants to know.

You sigh. 'Because,' you say, exactly as though the two of you have never had this conversation before, 'there are no men around.' The waitress comes over with your order. 'All the men I meet are either married, involved with someone, or gay.'

The waitress puts the Fresh Vegetable Plate in front

of you. 'Tell me about it,' she says.

Your mother is still where you left her. 'There's nothing wrong with a man being happy,' she says.

'Not happy, Mother. Homosexual.'

All the other diners who hadn't looked at you when you dropped the sugar or started to discuss your cystitis look at you now. You look down at the alfalfa sprouts. The waitress sets your mother's toasted cheese sandwich before her.

'Don't make excuses,' says your mother. 'There are plenty of eligible men around.'

The waitress sets down the condiment caddy. 'Where?'

You swallow a mouthful of low-fat cottage cheese. 'Oh yeah?'

'If you're not meeting them,' continues your mother, 'it's your own fault. Your expectations are too high. You always were too fussy. You get that from your father's side of the family. Nobody's perfect. Women have to compromise. Why don't you just make do like everybody else?' (It is interesting at this point to note that this advice is coming from a woman who, when you were younger, rejected every man you ever dated as not being good enough for you.)

Is your mother right? Is it all your fault? Are you too fussy? Do you have unreasonably high standards? Are you barring the door to your heart to perfectly acceptable men just because they have a few little surface flaws? Men who, for instance, wear white socks, loafers and gold chains? Men who in the company of other men and a few glasses of beer immediately start nudging each other and using terms like 'tits' and 'bazooms' and 'hot little number' and 'dying for it, absolutely dying for it' and 'what I could do with that tight little ass'? Men whose lips move when they read? Morticians? Used-car salesmen and politicians?

Do you hold it against a man just because when you make a rather clever joke about your uncle who is so obsessed with saving money by doing things himself that he wound up paying £10,000 to modernize the kitchen that a contractor would have done for five he not only doesn't laugh but asks you for an itemized list of what was done and what it cost?

Or do you, perhaps, have a low boredom threshold? Are you unable to concentrate on the finer details of the 1982 World Cup for longer than an hour and a half? After the fourth time that he's told you about his university or army days do you immediately start thinking of something else (what you'll have for breakfast, whether or not you should have bought that yellow scarf) whenever he says, 'Boy, I remember once …'? Did you never want to be an expert on the theory of dry fly fishing?

Are you too demanding? Do you think that if you have sat through the football season, the cricket season, the basketball season, the tennis season, and the hockey season, when nothing that didn't involve a ball being manhandled from one point to another was worthy of attention (well, maybe one thing), that it is not too much to expect him to go with you to have dinner with your friend from work?

In brief, do you have the wrong attitude? Do you have, in fact, an attitude that would make it difficult if not impossible for any flesh-and-blood man to win your heart? Not being the daughter of a king who likes to torture his child's suitors, is it you yourself who puts you on top of the glass mountain and then expects some poor fool to claw his way to the top? How many short guitar players with cute smiles do you think there are in New Jersey? Is it true, as Jane from time-to-time maintains, that not being able to lick the terrorists you have decided to join them and have become your very own saboteur?

What follows is a little quiz to help you determine just what your attitude to men and relationships with them really is.

The Are You Ready? Quiz

A. How do you feel about the following statements? We want your first, immediate response here, not what you've decided you feel after a two-hour telephone discussion with a friend who still has the first bridal bouquet she ever wrenched out of the hands of someone else wrapped in plastic at the bottom of her cupboard.

If God had meant women to live alone He wouldn't have created men.

1. True. Despite the fact that it is often difficult to tell from their behaviour that men belong to the same species as women, no one can deny that human beings need two sexes to carry out the Divine plan of procreation. If God hadn't intended these two sexes to live together one can assume that He would have made the earthworm and then quit while He was ahead.

2. False. God did mean women to live alone, and so He created men so as not to put too much temptation in her way. Such an unsuitable, unreliable, and generally bothersome companion was clearly designed for nothing more long-term than those few crucial minutes in the reproduction process when he actually has something to contribute.

3. True. Men may not always be without their little faults, but who is? There are just as many charming, warm, kind, sensitive, intelligent, and funny men who are good dancers as there are women. Men are nice to cuddle, handy when you need a push for the car, and endearing when put in charge of cats, iguanas, or small children.

A bird in the hand is worth two in the bush.

1. True. Even if there is always the chance that due to some fault of the travel agent's I'll miss my flight back from my holiday in Venice, get shifted to another plane and be put in first class instead of economy, thus finding myself sitting next to Harrison Ford, whose wife has just left him and who is desperate for the sympathy and understand-

ing of a natural brunette who is not involved in the hyper world of Hollywood, there is always the chance that things will go smoothly and I'll come back from Venice sandwiched between a rather nervous woman who is terrified of flying and keeps clutching my hand and a drunken businessman who falls flat on his face in the aisle when he gets up to go to the loo. With that in mind, it makes sense to check through the personal ads every weekend. And even more sense not to break up with Jeremy, even though he is a Dire Straits bore.

2. False. A bird in the hand is only worth two in the bush if the bird in the hand is one you want. If what you're interested in is a Pygmy Kingfisher, a Carrion Crow is not going to do you any good at all. This is the sort of advice your mother gives you after she's spent a sleepless night tossing and turning because she's just realized that your biological clock will soon be striking its eleventh hour.

3. True. The man I met at the Marks and Spencer wine tasting last month may not exactly be the sort of man I thought I would end up with when I was younger (he's a little shorter, a little less muscular, a little less hirsute, and I did sort of imagine that my ideal partner would have one or two more topics of conversation than himself), but he does have a steady job, own his own home, and drive a BMW. He is always punctual, even-tempered and shows a keen interest in doing my tax forms for me.

Beggars can't be choosers.

1. True. This does not mean, of course, that I have any intention of giving in to the advances of the mechanic at my garage who is always offering to

'look under the bonnet' for me as a personal favour. But it does mean that a person can be a little more flexible in her standards than she was. I would no longer rule out men who don't button up their shirts, men who look as though they spend the lonely hours between midnight and dawn making obscene phonecalls, or men who never go anywhere without their two Doberman Pinschers, Love and Hate (who, after all, can be sure that they don't indicate a very sophisticated sense of humour?). You can still be choosy, but you should first make sure that you have something to choose from.

2. False. Who says beggars can't be choosers? What sort of élitist, reactionary, anti-Christian bunk is that? And, anyway, who says I'm a beggar? I may not be Whitney Houston (a fact, I must admit, that is not one of the larger disappointments of my life), and I may not have been approached by a man since that drunk on the bus stop the night of the Royal Wedding, but I am still a unique and pretty wonderful person with a full and happy life. If I don't find the man who not only makes my heart race and my hormones tingle, but who also appreciates me for what and who I am, then why waste myself on second best? And at least it'll mean that I have more time to devote to saving the Amazonian rainforest.

3. True. Life is full of compromise. You want a Ferrari but you settle for a secondhand Ford. You want to go to Barbados for your summer holiday but you settle for Cornwall. What you really want for supper is a grilled pineapple, cheese, onion, avocado, tomato and chilli sandwich, but you don't go without eating just because the only thing in the house is a tin of vegetable soup and a handful of water biscuits. My mother, like Mick Jagger, always

impressed on me the fact that we can't always get what we want, and they were right. Once you become realistic about your expectations as regards finding a life-partner, you realize that there are quite a few available men around, and not all of them are violent.

Some women blame men for everything.

1. True. Men can, of course, be childish, self-centred, insensitive, and demanding. Many of them like to have things their own way. They don't always remember to put the milk away or to put their dirty dishes in the sink. They won't send you a birthday card or buy you a present, not only because they forget, but because they don't think it's important, even if you do. At the same time, however, they'll throw a wobbly if you forget that Saturday's the night they're televising the second round of the FA Cup and invite your parents over, because the FA Cup is important. Nonetheless, some women – though less, I think than there used to be – do go overboard and hold men responsible for every little thing that goes wrong in their lives. I mean, fair's fair. We've been on the planet as long as they have, after all.

2. True. Not that they don't have a point. 'What do you have against men?' men ask the critical female. 'Well,' she says, frowning thoughtfully, 'let's see. World War I? World War II? The nuclear bomb? A world economic system that favours the few and exploits the many? A global psychology that is based on power, fear and bigotry? Hitler? Stalin? Ghenghis Kahn? Ethiopia? Iran? Afghanistan? Bangladesh? Kampuchea? The Sudan? –' 'Oh, come on now,' they interrupt. 'Let's not go overboard, huh? You can't blame the entire history of the

human race on men.' 'But you guys always take all the credit,' she points out. 'No, no,' they say, standing firm, not the victims of their emotions as women are, 'you can't blame men for situations and leaders of which they were as much the pawns as anybody else.' 'Okay,' she says, taught by her mother always to be fair and agreeable and not give people a hard time. 'I don't want to be unjust. Let's look at it another way. How many rapists, muggers, child-abusers, wife-beaters, and serial killers have two X chromosomes?' 'Oh brother,' they groan, slapping their foreheads, 'you women really do blame us for everything.'

3. True. Men are people, after all, just as we are, and they do the best they can. If it weren't for men we'd all still be sitting in a cave in Central Africa, listening to the wolves howl outside and carving stick figures on the walls. We wouldn't have electricity or the jet plane or prepacked cheese or Nutra-Sweet or a multi-billion-pound defence industry. I think men should be thanked by women instead of being criticized all the time.

There is nothing lonelier than a vibrator.

1. True. Not that they don't have their uses, of course. Although it should be said that were the customs inspectors to go through your luggage at Moscow airport and discover a man tucked under the sweaters the man would probably be a lot easier and less embarrassing to explain than your deluxe portable vibrator. (In my experience, the customs men at Moscow seem a little unfamiliar with female things like tampons and those bendy rubber curlers, but even more sophisticated inspectors – with, perhaps, the exception of those at L.A. and Paris – have a tendency to behave oddly when confronted

with an instrument of carnal pleasure, especially if it comes with attachments, and even more especially if they have accidentally switched it on and it's whirring as they lift it into the light of day.) Aside from that advantage, men also talk and kiss and can often be persuaded to be the one who goes into the kitchen to rustle up the snack.

2. **False.** There are several things that have the potential of being lonelier than a vibrator, and most of them have two legs, grow facial hair, and have a pet name for their penis. One of these things was my first husband, Fred. No matter where you were, what time it was, or how much fun you'd been having, within three minutes of orgasm Fred would be sound asleep. (Nor was there any chance of waking him again for the next eight hours. Fred slept through an earthquake, a hurricane, most of the Woodstock Festival, and the small revolution that occurred on the romantic island where we'd gone for our honeymoon, most of which he also missed.) There you'd be, all aglow and still feeling frisky, his arms warm around you and in the middle of introducing some of your most secret thoughts and feelings into this moment of passion and intimacy, and all of a sudden you'd hear Fred snoring away like an old dog. There was never any chance of getting Fred to get up and make a snack. Instead, I'd just go and sit in the kitchen with the fridge door open and the late film on the television, telling Humphrey Bogart about what happened on the school picnic the year I was fourteen between mouthfuls of chocolate cake and cheese with chutney.

3. **True.** You ain't just whistlin' Dixie. The very thought of lying there all by yourself with this plastic thing like an obscene gesture makes me feel lonely. Even a man who thinks it's called foreplay

because it only lasts for four minutes is better than that. Even a man who makes you sleep in the wet patch is at least an improvement over something that runs on a battery. Even a man who can't remember your name has the advantage of being a little human company.

True love.

1. Well, more or less. Since the age of nine I've been in love with no less than forty-three men, including two university professors, John Lennon, my brother's best friend, Martin Millsteen, who became a priest in 1975, my gynaecologist, and the vet who gave the cat her operation. It's not that I don't believe in love, it's just that there are different degrees, and certainly a woman in her lifetime can fall in love with more than one man. It's a lot like fashion. One month you're using the rent money to buy that orange cocktail dress made out of parachute silk, and the next you're using that orange cocktail dress to mop up the bathroom floor. Love's very similar. You spend five years of your life absolutely apeshit in love with Darwin, a gorgeous and successful divorce lawyer who wears Armani suits and has more girlfriends than Cadburys has got chocolates, you go into deep, two-pizzas-and-a-bottle-of-tequila depressions when he doesn't call you for a week or forgets you had a date, you forgive him his indiscretions and don't complain when he goes off to Bali for a month to rediscover himself and leaves you watering the plants and walking the Yorkshire terrier, you listen to Billie Holiday records till four in the morning and tell yourself that you will die if Darwin isn't at least a small part of your life (and vice versa) every time you discover he's been out with someone else – and

then, just when Darwin is showing real signs of getting serious about you, you discover that you're in love with an Irish flute player of small stature and limited career prospects but a five-hundred-watt smile. That's true love.

2. True. A person is lucky if she falls really in love even once in her life. And it is, of course, easy to confuse love with infatuation, or lust, or panic, or even temporary madness. But it definitely does exist. And it isn't based on any of the things that infatuation, lust, panic, or even madness are based on (looks, propinquity, money, power, loneliness, a hereditary weakness for skinny men with aqua-blue eyes, animal magnetism, peer or familial pressure, outside expectations and demands ...), it just is. Like quantum physics, it isn't something that lends itself to any easy explanation: you have to take it on trust. The only real problem with true love (aside from the fact that its appearances are infrequent and often badly timed) is that just because it exists between two people doesn't mean that they'll be able to live together any more happily than two people who aren't in love. Look at Richard and Liz, to name but a few. Look at me and Larry Kalinski. Whew. He came into the record shop where I was working and asked me for an old Dave Van Ronk album. 'It's the one with "Candy Man" on it,' he said, as our eyes met. I could barely remember my name, never mind the name of the record. Larry moved in two days later (that is to say that two days later he left my flat for three hours to go and organize the transportation of his belongings). Larry and I couldn't be within a hundred yards of one another without being overwhelmed with physical passion. In crowds we only saw each other. An hour away from Larry Kalinski was like a day, a day like a year, etc. I couldn't remember how

I had existed without him. He couldn't imagine how he had existed without me. We had been fated for each other, and we knew it. Through the centuries we had struggled separately until at last we came to the time and place of our meeting. And what happened? As much as I loved Larry, I couldn't stand his personal habits. He cut his nails in bed. He left his dirty socks under the cushions in the living room. If you put your fork down for a minute he'd finish your meal. As much as Larry loved me, my practical jokes drove him crazy. He hated my cooking. He couldn't tolerate my tendency to tidy things up all the time. We fought about everything. We fought about who used the stereo last and who was supposed to do the shopping for supper. We fought about his parents, and my parents, and whether or not the cat (his cat) should be declawed. We fought about Christmas and whether or not *Catch-22* could be considered a major literary work. We argued about the right way to tie the laces on your shoes. I still dream and yearn for Larry Kalinski, but in my heart of hearts I know that if I ran into him tomorrow the first thing he'd say to me would be, 'I'd have recognized you anywhere. As usual, you're inappropriately dressed for the weather'; and the first thing I'd say to him would be, 'Larry, you look gorgeous, but what's all that gunk on your sleeve?'

3. In a way. I certainly believe in love, but love is built out of friendship, compatibility, having things in common, and mutual respect. It doesn't hit you like some bolt from the blue. It has to be worked at. Helped to grow. Nurtured. I like to think of it as rather like making your way in the property market. Your father gives you a little money as a graduation present and you use it as a downpayment on a tiny one-bedroom flat half a mile from the nearest bus or

tube, in a neighbourhood that hasn't started to become fashionable and has probably never seen better days. A few years later, you sell that flat at an absolutely enormous profit and you move into a three-bedroom house with a garden. With love what happens is you meet someone in whom you're interested, and so forth, and you begin to date. You get to know each other gradually, over a period of time. If you don't see each other for a week or two you don't spend every night on the telephone to your best friend, crying and eating your way through packets of chocolate digestives and family-size bags of crisps, and he doesn't leave heartsick messages on your answering machine. When you go on holiday you send him a postcard, and when he goes on holiday he brings you back a cute little egg cosy that says Rio on it. In time, he realizes that whenever he wants to go hear African music you are the person he asks along, and you realize that it is he who escorts you to all your friends' weddings and large celebrations. You start talking about your relationship. You decide to go away together for a week. That works pretty well (you are not over-the-moon to discover that he takes three showers a day and always eats garlic for lunch, but you can live with it). You decide to move in together. In time, you buy some new furniture together and a new car and you have a new kitchen fitted, and then the boiler explodes, which brings you even closer together, and then one day when you're holding the ladder while he hangs the new curtains, he looks down at you, dedicatedly protecting his life, and he says, 'What do you think, old girl? Should we tie the knot?' And there you have it, forty years of wedded bliss and a retirement home in the country.

B. Select the answer that best describes how you would react in the following situations. Be honest, the angels are watching.

1. It has been a long, cold winter. You have been working too hard and having little fun – unless you count the weekend you visited your old school chum and her family in the country (where you learned considerably more about breast feeding and the difficulties of heating charming period cottages than you had ever wanted to know) fun. Over the past few years, a series of disastrous relationships has left you with the suspicion that if there is a perfect mate for you somewhere on this planet he is probably in prison in Guatemala. In all other respects, however, your life is good and often even excellent. But as contented and well-balanced as you are in general, those winter blues have set in and you sometimes find yourself staring into windows of travel agencies, wondering about Tunisia. Nonetheless, you have made it into February, and spring, where, as everyone knows, hope blooms eternal, is hovering on the horizon. But, of course, you forgot: though a short month, February has right in its middle the one holiday meant only for couples. St Valentine's Day. Last year you managed to escape it by going on a business trip to Cracow (not a city made for lovers), but this year no such refuge is in sight. Your horoscope says that Saturn is in transit and that you should be careful, though it doesn't specify of what. It is late on Friday afternoon when a work friend, who is rumoured to have a jacuzzi, invites you to a Valentine's Day fancy dress party the following night. Guests have to dress as some famous lover of history or literature. This friend assures you that everyone who has been invited is interesting, intelligent and exciting to be with (which would be

a party first), and that you will have the best of times. You

a. Think this sounds like just the ticket. Remembering the fancy dress party in *The Pink Panther*, you see this as an opportunity for fun, flirtation, possible romance, and even adventure. It certainly beats watching the special on endangered species on Channel 4, as you had planned. On the way home from work you stop off and buy a long black wig with a fringe and a gold lamé bra. You have already decided to go as Cleopatra.

b. Put up several objections. You don't really like parties. You were planning to get started on painting the kitchen tomorrow night. You haven't worn a costume since you played one of the workhouse boys in your primary school's performance of *Oliver Twist*. Your friend, however, whose nickname in the office is Gruppenführer Davies, is not inclined to take no for an answer. 'Don't be such an old stick in the mud,' she says. 'You're not getting any younger, you know. Who do you think is going to want you when you're old and grey? If you don't get out and about now, you're going to find yourself all alone with a shawl, a hot water bottle and fifteen stray cats. You'll end up spending your last years in some old people's home with turquoise walls and artificial flowers on the table at Christmas, without even a few happy memories to keep you company. Think of that.' Under the weight of such a persuasive argument, you decide that, maybe the kitchen can wait another week. On the way home from work you stop off and buy some black felt and a length of red and white polka dot material. You have already decided to go as Minnie Mouse.

c. In 1979, at a fancy dress party whose theme was Ancient Rome (which produced quite a few guys with violins, several gladiators, a preponderance of dancing girls and pouting, nubile slaves, and one chap with a styrofoam cross), you met Steve. Steve was dressed as a lion, which you took as a sign of cleverness and wit. As it turned out, all it was a sign of was that Steve's flatmate (who was clever and witty) had loaned it to him to prevent Steve from wrapping himself in a sheet and sticking a few bay leaves behind his ear. Steve, however, even in a mane and tail, was gorgeous, and your pheromones shouted a lot louder than the voice of caution. By the time you figured out that when the brains were handed out Steve had been in the bathroom, looking in the mirror, you and he were already sharing a flat. Because Steve was, in truth, a very sweet guy who loved you almost as much as he loved himself, the break-up was a long and painful one, and ended with you throwing every mirror in the house into the back garden. Ever since, you have been, like a vampire, shy of reflecting surfaces, and, also like a vampire, not too keen on fancy dress parties. Therefore, you don't even think twice about accepting this invitation. 'Oh, no!' you exclaim. 'I can't believe it! What a shame. Tomorrow's the night Bob Dylan's coming over for supper. I'd bring him along, but you know how reclusive and moody he is.'

2. It is a bleak and stormy night. You are sitting on an orange plastic chair in your local Chinese take-away, debating with yourself whether to have your usual (fried rice and sweet and sour prawns) or whether you should treat yourself to something daring and exotic (Singapore noodles or paper-wrapped chicken). Suddenly, the man two seats

over – the only other intrepid diner out on this wild, ferocious night – leans towards you and whispers, 'Excuse me, Miss. But would you happen to know what Moo Gai Pan is?' You hadn't noticed anything about this man before, except for the puddle his Doc Martin's are making on the patches of cardboard that have been laid down by the management to protect the lino, but now you see that he isn't completely unattractive. He has a nice smile (though so, of course, does Warren Beatty). His one gold earring is rather sexy. He does not look like either an accountant or a psychiatrist. Though his hands are still in their wool gloves (not, you assume, because he is about to rob the place but because the take-away is a little on the chilly side), they are large and look as though they are probably quite remarkable. He could be a painter or a musician (which you think would make him interesting). You

a. Drop your menu onto your lap and turn to him with your warmest smile. 'Oh, Moo Gai Pan,' you enthuse, 'now isn't that a clever idea. I always wind up with something that can be reheated the next day in case the portion's too much for just one person. Does your wife like pork?'

b. Can't for the life of you remember what Moo Gai Pan is, but you think it involves pancakes. In your anxiety to explain to him the complexities of rolling up the pancakes so that the sauce and filling don't fall on the table, you knock your handbag on the floor. While he's bending down to help you pick up your change, your address book, your keys, two empty tissue packets, an assortment of old make-up, a teaspoon, half a Kit Kat, one tampon (miraculously enough still in its wrapper), three combs (one of them for an Afro), a well-used hairbrush and a tube of deodorant you recommend the sweet and sour prawns. 'It's what I always get,' you mumble.

c. Turn to him with a baffled if not actually hostile expression on your face. 'I haven't the slightest idea,' you say. 'It sounds like some guy who was purged in the Cultural Revolution.'

3. Lo and behold, here you are on your way to the St Valentine's party. Because of a sudden lack of self-confidence that has a lot to do with what your mother would say about your chances of getting pneumonia if she saw you in your costume, you decide not to risk public transport. You order a mini cab. Even though you've got your old trench coat clasped around you, the driver watches your approach with undisguised interest, bordering on admiration. As it turns out, he is not really a mini-cab driver at all, but a promising young playwright with eyes just like Paul Newman's. He goes off duty in twenty minutes.

a. Although you were carefully brought up not to talk to strangers, not to take rides from strangers, and certainly not to go out drinking with strangers when you're dressed as though you just got off work as either an exotic dancer or a mouse, your reasoning is that if you don't do these things with strangers you won't do them with anyone. If you went to the party you would still wind up with a stranger (theoretically), and in this case you at least know where he works.

b. There is no way you're going to saunter into the Prince of Wales dressed as you are, and you're certainly not going to go to his place when you haven't actually seen the colour of his eyes in even artificial light. So you bring him to the party with you, telling everyone that he's supposed to be Stanley Kowalski.

c. You get out of the cab. You get out of the cab, and then you wait forty-five minutes for a bus, during which time it begins to snow. Two people come up to you asking for directions, one person comes up to you asking for money, and one person pulls up to the kerb in a powder-blue Mercedes and offers you fifty pounds. You decide that God is trying to tell you that He would have been a lot more pleased with you if you'd stayed home and learned about the plight of the dolphins – and so home you go.

4. It is a well-known fact that more people commit suicide on a Sunday afternoon in mid-winter than on any other single day, including Christmas. You, I am happy to say, did not commit suicide, but you did come close. You found yourself answering one of the ads in the personals:

> Rosie Come Out Tonight. HERE I AM – and THERE YOU ARE. We don't know each other but if we did we could rock all night, watch old movies, drink tequilas and watch the sun rise – and maybe even fall in love. Let's roll down the windows and let the wind blow back our hair.

Now here you are, headed for your first meeting with a man who described himself in his letter as a quiet, stable professional man with a blazing soul.

Clark Kent on the outside and David Coverdale on the inside. You are meeting him outside Macdonald's. He thought it was a clean and convenient meeting place, unthreatening and familiar to both of you. He will be wearing a blue corduroy jacket and an Elvis badge, and you will be wearing a short black skirt and cowboy boots. You

a. Show up on time and walk right up to him, undaunted by the fact that he looks far more on the quiet than the blazing side. You can't judge a book by its cover (as Lois Lane discovered), you remind yourself. Plenty of tall, handsome, exciting-looking men are about as interesting as a tunafish sandwich on white bread, crusts removed. In fact, you and he spend a very pleasant if less than fiery evening listening to him talk about his job (although he really wanted to be a rhythm guitarist he makes artificial limbs for a living; you agree that life is strange the way it sometimes works out) and his favourite music (most of it written after 1948). He behaves like a gentleman, pays for your cheeseburger and fries, and invites you to a movie in a week's time. 'If we go past Music City I can show you the guitar I was going to buy if my group hadn't broken up in 1978,' he says as he walks you to the train (where, no doubt, the windows have already been rolled down). You say, 'Oh, that sounds great.'

b. Just to be on the safe side, you wear your basketball sneakers instead of the cowboy boots and pin up your hair. He is not quite what you'd expected from his ad (he is more reminiscent of Rick Astley than Bruce Springsteen), but on the other hand he doesn't look as though he molests small children, and he seems to be sober (a great improvement on your last boyfriend). You go to a bar with a great jukebox, and you are suitably impressed by his ability to name every member of every band. When he says, 'Shhh, listen to that riff –' (although you were not, as it happens, talking) '– it's just like the one Alex Yates did on the bootleg 1958 version of "Sick City Blues",' you say, 'Oh, do you think so? I sort of thought it reminded me of Duane Allman on "Statesboro Blues", you know, from the Fillmore East Album.' He gazes at you with a new look in his eyes and glances at his watch.

c. You wear jeans and your old reindeer sweater and walk five times around the block before guilt (if you've come this far, what's the point of not continuing?; the poor guy is standing there, shaking his watch every few seconds and trying not to look as though he thinks he's been stood up; your friends will tease you for the next eighteen months when they find out that despite all their years of advice and counselling you still act as though you're twelve) propels you beneath the golden arches. Well, there he is and here you are. As you idly dip your fries into your shake while he entertains you with the simply incredible story of a man whose artificial hand was so real-looking that his wife didn't realize it was a replacement part until the night it fell off during an especially vigorous bout of lovemaking (heh heh), you reflect on the relativity of time, where an hour playing pool with Tom Cruise would seem like a minute, and a minute with a failed guitarist whose special sauce keeps slipping out of his burger seems like about forty years.

5. No single person in her right mind would do her grocery shopping at any time but late Friday night.

For it is late on a Friday night that the family shoppers are safely tucked up in front of the television and the one-adult, two-cat households have the place to themselves. No children constantly knocking pyramids of cereal boxes on top of you or trying to get hit by your trolley. No women with babies strapped to their backs and toddlers mixed in with the foodstuffs and household goods looking at you pityingly as you put your single-serving packets and your half a head of cabbage on the counter. But even though you know all this, here you are on a Saturday morning, with a dinner party to shop for, a mother of a hangover, and a face that hasn't set yet, bravely and not too successfully negotiating the obstacles in the fruit and vegetables aisle. You are wedged between a pillar and the Ugli Fruit, trying to find a plastic bag holder that still has some plastic bags on it, when a pretty presentable bloke who looks as though this may be his first time in active combat leans towards you (causing a minor landslide of lychees) and asks in a nervous whisper how you can tell if a pineapple is ripe. You

a. Check that he isn't wearing a wedding ring or a little pink triangle, and offer to demonstrate. By the time you have both been severely cut by pineapple fronds, you have exchanged not only recipes but phone numbers as well.

b. Nimbly step over the lychees on the floor and make your way to the pineapples, where you quickly find one that's ripe for him. He can't thank you enough. He usually doesn't eat pineapples since he can never tell if they're ripe or not, but he woke up this morning with this sudden urge, you know? You do know about sudden urges, but even though his smile is a lot warmer than your electric blanket, and there is no evidence from the things in his basket that he is either a big eater or shopping for two, you do nothing more than say, 'Well, I hope you enjoy the pineapple,' and return to the hunt for a bag.

c. Sigh audibly. Men. Here you are with a pound of carrots clutched under your armpit and he wants you to tell him if the bloody pineapple's ready or not. Why can't they ever do anything for themselves? You'd think a grown man would to be able to buy himself a piece of fruit without any outside help. It's not as though people only eat every once in a while. 'I wouldn't know,' you say shortly. 'I always buy them in tins.'

6. It is a chill and rainy Friday night, and you have been standing huddled under the bus shelter for more than half an hour, wondering what possessed you to go out on a night like this just because you had a sudden craving for the cheese burritos and extra-hot salsa served at Lil's Cafe. To while away the hours while you wait for the bus, you have been playing the What If Game (what if Jeff Bridges were to come along right now and offer you a lift; what if war was suddenly declared; what if armed gunmen were to hold up the 7-Eleven behind you; what if you were to look down and see a stray Prussian Blue kitten; what if you won the pools; etc.). You are just working out what would happen if Eric Clapton were to come up to you right now, asking if you knew where the fabulous Caribbean restaurant he's heard so much about is, when you realize that someone is talking to you. It isn't, alas, Eric Clapton, but it is a rather attractive gentleman who seems

surprised that he has never seen you on this bus stop before. 'Do you come here often?' he would like to know.

a. An avid reader of women's magazines, you are able to size him up in under four seconds. He is obviously a man with a good job, good education, and great social skills. He is positive, friendly, fun to be with, and a man of true discretion and taste. Though he is a little drunk, because while out shopping for things for his birthday party on Sunday he ran into a few friends who wanted to celebrate early, he is clearly intelligent, has a good sense of humour (he responds well to your joke about buses in the rain), and is caring and responsible (you can tell this because his shoes are polished, though, to be honest, in this downpour everything looks pretty polished). You are just hoping that his bus doesn't come for a while so that you have a chance to get to know him a little when, as is the way with these things, his bus comes chugging around the corner. His bus does not go anywhere near Lil's Cafe. If you get on his bus you will end up miles out of your way, and in a neighbourhood not known for being particularly friendly towards lone women after dark. Your new friend smiles at you. It's as though someone just turned on a spotlight. 'Going my way?' he quips. You say, 'Yes. What a coincidence!'

b. You are a little shy about striking up conversations with drunken strangers on bus stops late on a rainy Friday night. Even when the stranger in question is a man you would be delighted to talk to if you had met, say, at a friend's house or over those little bits of puff pastry filled with dead fish at a party. You do assure him that you often come to this bus stop. 'Imagine that,' he says. 'And I've never met you before.' He then invites you to his birthday party on Sunday. 'Oh, that's very nice of you,' you say, and rummage in your bag for an old receipt on whose back he can write his address. 'One o'clock on Sunday,' he says. You say you'll try to make it. Just then his bus comes around the corner on two wheels. 'Do you take this bus, too?' he asks as it skids to a halt. You could take it, but it would mean changing buses after he got off. 'No,' you say, wishing your mother had been of a slightly more bohemian nature, 'no I don't.' As he swings onto the bus, he shouts out, 'Don't forget! One o'clock on Sunday!' You carry his name and address around in your purse for a week.

c. All you want at this moment in time is to be warm and dry and tucking into a bowl of tortilla soup. You are sick to death of men thinking they can just walk up to a woman they have never seen before and treat her as though she's got a For Sale sign stuck to her forehead. You are fed up with male egotism that says that a woman who is standing on a bus stop, minding her own business and thinking her own thoughts, should feel flattered that some guy who smells like Saturday night at the Crown and Garter wants to tell her all about himself. You pull yourself up to your full height, look him straight in his Bambi-brown eyes, smile sweetly, and say, 'I am carrying a loaded revolver, Mister, and I'm not afraid to use it.'

How to score

In section A., give yourself two points for every 1. you gave as your response; one point for every 2.; and three points for every 3. In section B., give yourself three points for every a.; two points for every b.; and one point for every c.

If you have scored a mere eleven points, then the chances are that you are more likely to spend your time taking self-defence classes than flattening your tummy. You are not a person who goes in for nonsense, or pinches of salt, or smoothing down your principles to get through the rockier passes of life. You think we're all adults and that's the way we should both behave and be treated. My mother would not like to be on trial with you on the jury. You have, in fact, an attitude that my mother (for one) would describe as 'just like Aunt Enid'. One fine spring day when they were young and arrestingly beautiful, Aunt Enid and her twin sister, my mother, were walking through the park when a very handsome and charming man somewhat older than they approached them. He said something like, 'My my, it isn't every day that one finds oneself in the company of such beautiful twins.' My mother smiled (in Aunt Enid's version, my mother simpered). Aunt Enid said, 'You're not in our company, you're by yourself.' The man, undaunted by this lack of encouragement, went on about the lovely day and the great coffee served at this cafe he knew not all that far away and how he would like to talk to them some more. My mother, who was sure she knew this handsome and charming man from somewhere and was constantly nudging the unresponsive Enid to tell her this, said, 'Well ...', but Enid, the elder by five minutes she was never going to forget, said, simply, 'We do not talk to men who try to pick us up in the park,' and dragged her sister away. It was only as they were taking their seats in the bus heading home that my mother slapped herself in the forehead and cried out, 'Oh my goodness, I just realized who that was! Oh, Enid, you dope, that was Cary Grant!' and, shoving her beloved sister into the lap of yet another strange man, tried to jump off a moving vehicle.

If you have scored between eleven and sixteen, you've still been spending a great deal of your free time reading Dale Spender and Marilyn French, but there are tiny chinks of light in the armour. All those years of being conditioned to believe that love and marriage, a solid relationship and a family, are more important to you than anything else – that no matter what else is happening in your life you are not complete until you are part of a couple – have not been totally in vain. We all have days when we feel like we must be the only single person in the world, if not the solar system, when everywhere you go there are couples licking each other in public, or hanging on to one another for dear life, or calling across the store to each other, 'Darling, what do you think about this one on me?', while you try to give yourself an objective evaluation of how the purple hat with the little black pompons really looks on you, taking into account that when you wear it to your cousin's wedding you will not be dressed in overalls and a workshirt. Days when we wander past wine bars and restaurants and see all the smiling, laughing, canoodling couples, wondering why we have been singled out to be the only person left alone. But your days are coming more often and closer together. If you were to engage in a little aversion therapy (for instance, answering one personal ad a week, always turning up, and never leaving halfway through the date on the grounds that you have suddenly started to haemorrhage; or, even better, go out of your way at least once a fortnight to ask a man for advice. Ask the man in the garage what an

automatic choke is and how it works. Ask your
brother-in-law how venture capitalism works. When
he says, 'This isn't boring you, is it?' say, 'Boring me?
How could something that has brought so much good
to mankind be boring me? – if you do this, you might,
in time, be ready to date seriously.

A score of between sixteen and twenty-three means
that though your flesh is pretty willing your spirit is
still on the reluctant side. You would like to get out
there and hunt, but you have been living on your own
too long and have a well-entrenched sense of pride
and self. You'll get all dressed up in your heels and
leather dress and go with the girls to the trendy
watering hole, but after the third wine-bar cowboy
comes up to you and starts a conversation about
French cheese or how much money he's going to make
in the next twelve months you start yawning and
thinking about what you'd be doing if you were at
home. Remember how long it took you in your piano
lessons before you managed to master '*Claire de la
Lune*'?

Between twenty-three and twenty-nine? Now that's
the sort of spirit the future grandparents of your
children like to see. You are sensible, mature, and
though obviously quite capable of taking care of
yourself, you are also obviously quite capable of taking
care of someone else as well. You show initiative,
imagination, and a willingness to give men all the
attention they assume they deserve – feminine traits
that have been perfected over the centuries, ever since
the first cavewoman, having lured the great elk into
the ravine in the first place, then sat around the
campfire for the next twelve nights, smiling and
nodding and saying, 'You were wonderful, Ugbug',
while he talked about his great hunting skills and drew
pictures of himself in various spearing postures on the
wall.

Twenty-nine to thirty-four? You are definitely ready.

You leave no stone unturned, and show an exemplary positiveness in your approach to men. No nagging little doubts, no residual bad-feelings here. No harking back to so-and-so who ran off with your sister or what-was-his-name who ran off with your savings and the car. No snap judgements and no defensiveness, just an approach that says: if he's out there, I'm going to find him – whether he wants to be found or not.

5

THE 'AIN'T-LIFE-A-BITCH' SYNDROME

Over the years, it has been pointed out by more than one person that the difference between men and children is largely one of size and method. Men are bigger than children and far less likely to throw themselves down on the floor of the department store, kicking and screaming and turning red in the face, because you won't buy them a watch that looks like a toad or a chocolate sundae. If a man suddenly climbs onto your lap, throws his arms around your neck and collapses against you with a sigh, the chances are he is not afraid of the lightning or suddenly overcome with affection for you, but merely very drunk. And when a man says he loves you he could, in fact, mean a variety of things (I want to go to bed with you; I don't want to go to bed with you; I want you to stop giving me a hard time; I'm having an affair with someone else who is prettier than you; I feel guilty for coming home at three in the morning when you've been sitting at the dining room table with the candles dwindling and the champagne growing warm since eight o'clock, waiting to celebrate your new job; and so forth), but when a child says she or he loves you, you know exactly where you stand.

All that aside, men and children do share certain characteristics and behaviour patterns. They both like a lot (and usually more than their fair share) of attention. You have had a killer of a day at work, meeting the Malaysian Minister of the Environment to discuss the destruction of Sarawak and being told that he, personally, wouldn't mind if the rainfall were to decrease because of deforestation because he, personally, doesn't think there are enough good golfing days as it is. After this, you had several smaller but no less frustrating confrontations, a major blowout with a co-worker over the funding of the tea and coffee, had to rewrite a twenty-page project proposal, stepped on your glasses (there is an explanation for their being on the floor of your office, but it probably isn't worth going into here), and remembered, during one of those suddenly free thirty seconds in the afternoon, that you still haven't sent off your mother's birthday card. On the way home from work, you arrive at the optician's two minutes after they've closed, march half a mile in the opposite direction to collect the dry cleaning (half of which, inexplicably, 'How do I know, lady? I just work the counter', isn't ready), pick up some things for supper, stop off at the self-service car wash and clean the car (forgetting, as one sometimes does, to put the aerial down). When you finally get home, a man will greet you with, 'Hello darling, wait'll I tell you what happened today,' and then proceed to tell you what happened today while you unpack the groceries and start scrounging in the fridge for the pasta salad you were saving for supper, which he, feeling peckish, has already eaten. If, after years of practice, you managed to say 'Hello darling, wait'll I tell you what happened today' before he could, he will start glancing at the newspaper or reading the ingredients on the yoghurt container while you talk, and then, while your head's in the fridge and your mind has switched for a few seconds from the global environmental crisis to why the blue bowl is no longer on the middle shelf, he will say quickly, 'Gee, honey that does sound pretty bad, but wait'll you hear what happened to me. Remember I was telling you about that idiot in accounts? ...' Or when you finally get home, a child will greet you with, 'Mummy! Mummy! Wait'll I tell you what happened today,' and then proceed to tell you what happened today while you unpack the groceries and feed the cat and pick up the articles of clothing and odd pieces of toys your child has left scattered all over the floor. Just as you are on your knees in front of the fridge, wondering why you can't see the blue bowl with the pasta salad in it (is this the first sign of senile dementia?), and your child is saying, 'No, no, that's not Jimmy Murphy, Jimmy Murphy is the one who cried when the girls hid his lunch box, why don't you listen to anything I tell you?', your child's father will suddenly appear in the doorway, shouting, 'What in hell have you done to the car?'

Men and children are equally sensitive to minor illnesses and injuries (the mild headache, the banged hand, the stomachache from mixing chocolate and chips or bourbon and wine), liable to take to the sofa in need of cold compresses and cups of tea and someone to offer assurances that death is not imminent and that there's chocolate custard for dessert for anyone who survives. Men and children do not like doing yukky things like cleaning out the swing bin or changing the cat litter or mopping up sick or fishing out things that fell in the toilet. Men and children do not like waiting around while you chat to a friend you just bumped into or try on just one more swimming costume. They hate it when you talk on the telephone at a time when you are supposed to be playing with them. They think that if you're sitting down it means you're waiting for someone to give you something to do. Both men and children are given to tantrums, though in the case of the latter you usually both say you're sorry in the end, and in the case of the former only you say you're sorry.

Another thing men and children have in common is the fact that they are both examples of what is universally known as the 'ain't-life-a-bitch' syndrome. For instance, strange as it may sound, many mothers spend their child's early years wishing that said child would go away. Not permanently, of course, but now and then, for a month or two, on a regular basis. They look back with fondness and a sigh for lost innocence to the days when they believed that children were cute little people who looked adorable when dressed up and who always said something funny or precious. They look back with nostalgia to the days when they themselves were free to boogie till dawn, when there weren't certain friends they couldn't visit because of their oriental carpets or their collection of antique glassware, when they didn't expect to be woken at the crack of dawn by the sound of a sweet little voice saying, 'Mummy, come and see what Dougie did'. Remembering the years they took for granted – the years when they were never afraid of finding a newt in the shower, when it wasn't necessary to lock themselves in the loo to get ten minutes of privacy, when they had time to read books besides *Hop, Little Kangaroo!* – they want to cry. And then what happens? Then, against all odds, the child grows up. Slowly, at first, but surely just the same. No sooner has mum resigned herself to the fact that she can never be alone, can't so much as run around the corner for a pint of milk without being trailed by short people on roller skates, the child makes friends of her or his own. All of a sudden there is no one to watch *Mork and Mindy* re-runs with. No one to hide Easter eggs for. No one to melt the butter while you pop the corn. They get so old and grown up that they not only don't bother to tell you where they're going, they never even suggest a time when they might be back. And you, of course, instead of celebrating the fact that after fourteen years it is at last possible to run through the house naked and have sex in the kitchen, begin to miss them. You want them around. You yearn for the days when you were on duty 336 hours a week, when they told you everything that happened to them every single day, from doing a wee to having a fight at break with Sally Killane over the skipping rope.

It's just the same with men.

You live with Stan for six years. And for six years he drives you crazy. Even though he has lived in the flat as long as you have, he can never remember where the coffee or the tin opener are kept, and even though he is a nuclear physicist of some distinction he has yet to work out the complexities of the washing machine. If you go away for a weekend, it is guaranteed that when you return you will discover that Stan has run out of toilet paper, milk and cat food while you were gone and that it has not occurred to him that he is permitted to replace them (so the cats are eating tinned tuna, last week's colour supplement is in the bog, and the fridge contains one empty milk carton). Despite all this, Stan is a fussbudget. If you leave something on the table (other than the coffee or the tin opener) he will put it away. If you put the newspaper to one side because there was something you wanted to read in it he will throw it out. If you put out the cheese dip to reach room temperature before the guests arrive, Stan will put it back in the fridge so that you have to serve it with knives instead of celery sticks. Stan is also a workaholic hypochondriac, torn between spending all his spare time doing the 'just a few things' he brought home from the office and taking his temperature and pulse. In many ways, living with Stan is like being alone – but with none of the benefits (you can't eat toast in bed because it makes him break out in a rash; you can't play your Talking Heads albums because it disturbs his concentration; you can't stay out too late on your own because it causes him anxiety). A typical evening with Stan consists of you rushing home to fix a meal that he doesn't eat because he works late and isn't hungry by the time he slumps through the door, or because someone left a copy of *Your Health Today* on the train and he now realizes that he's allergic to wheat. Then Stan will lock himself away to work, unless you have something you wanted to do, in which case he is overcome with the need to spend some time with you. And Stan is very competitive. He is a bad Scrabble loser, the sort of man who quibbles over the rules and re-checks the scores. If you say that 'Lola' came out in 1969 and he says that it came out in 1970, he will leave no stone unturned and no record shop uncalled in proving you are wrong (and on every occasion for the next few months that someone introduces music into the conversation, Stan will immediately say, 'My God, speaking of that, did I tell you what she came out with the other day? She ... she thought 'Lola' came out in 1969 ...'). Because he gets restless on weekends, when he is locked out of his lab on Sunday, holidays with Stan are few, brief, and far between – and normally spent with him felled by food poisoning, sunstroke, or a sensitivity to foreign water, even if it comes in bottles, and you staying close by in case he needs something (so that, though you and Stan have been to some of the world's great beauty spots, in your memory they all meld into one medium-sized hotel room with a view of the car park or the swimming pool). And, because he is always punctual, the number of times he has left you standing on a streetcorner or outside of the theatre are almost as numerous as the times you have come racing into the restaurant to find him sitting with his watch in his hand, counting the minutes.

Eventually, you and Stan come to the parting of the ways and the dinner set. You divide the dishes and the books and the records, you take the sheets and he takes the towels, and there you are, alone at last. You can play Paul Butterfield at full volume. Mucous foods and sugar are welcome in your home once more. The next time you go on vacation you will actually get to see the beach, eat shellfish, and order a cocktail ('I don't care what they say,' Stan always said, 'I don't trust the ice').

And what happens? Do you start throwing wild parties for windsurfers? Do you start serving raw salmon and water imported from a small village in Spain? Do you leave your socks on the dining-room table? Do you let the cat sleep in the fruit bowl? No. What happens is, you catch yourself using the tea bag twice. You suddenly discover that you really like muesli for breakfast, and not the high-cholesterol fry-up you'd previously favoured. Every time you leave a room you turn out the light. Your friends are suddenly unwilling to play Scrabble with you any more because you've become such a nit-picker, dragging the game out for hours while you re-count scores and look up every word in the *Oxford Unabridged*. You find yourself sitting up in bed, sipping Peaceful Evening herbal tea and watching the late film, but instead of concentrating on Chevy Chase (who is certainly worth the effort) you are wondering if Stan is sleeping well or if his insomnia's back; you almost think you can hear him sniffling in the other room. You can't quite get yourself to fill that space in the fridge where his shoebox of vitamins used to go.

Even if you and Stan don't get back together, it won't be long before you start looking for someone else to drive you nuts.

6

SOME WOMEN PREFER PETS

I have several friends and at least three close female relatives who find it impossible to appreciate this point of view. 'Don't be ridiculous,' their spokeswoman scoffs. 'It may be true that Aunt Cynthia got on a lot better with the bearded collie she bought after Uncle Simon passed away than she ever did with Uncle Simon, but I don't see that that proves anything. Almost everyone who ever knew him would have preferred a tree toad to Simon.' No matter what my mother says, however, there are many women who would rather have a budgerigar than a live-in boyfriend.

You can't imagine why?

Well, for one thing, a pet is no stickler for physical perfection. It does not, for example, care if your feet don't touch the floor when you sit on the kitchen chair or if you've been on a diet for fifteen years and still wouldn't like to be buried in stretch pants. A pet will not pinch your bottom while you're doing the dishes and inform you that he likes you on the plump side, just like Miss Piggy. Though it can be a little strange at first, sharing your bed with someone whose tail thumps against your arm and whose whiskers get up your nose, there is no chance that your cat is ever going to turn to you and say, 'Would you mind sleeping in the spare-room till your cold's better? You smell like Vicks.' If a pet comes into the bathroom in the morning and finds you standing on the scales, sobbing, the pet will not tell you that your trouble is that you don't think thin (like he does). A pet won't dismiss you as a friend and companion because your hair is thin or your teeth are crooked or you're not a redhead. Never once in the history of civilization has a cat, dog, or hamster been known to turn to the person who has shown it nothing but affection, consideration, love and understanding, and say, 'I'm sorry, Lucretia, but I just can't go on seeing someone who looks so much like a Cabbage Patch Doll.' Most pets (with the exceptions, perhaps, of tortoises and pigeons) are there when you need them. A man, confronted with your desperate tears, is just as likely to storm from the house with a brusque 'I'm going out' and a contemptuous sneer as he is to take you in his arms and try to comfort you. A dog, however, even if only that morning you yelled at him for being on the bed or fed him liver-flavoured food for breakfast when you know he can't stand it, will come over and sit beside you and put his head on your knee, as if to say, 'I know there's nothing anyone can say to make you feel better, but I want you to know that you are not alone, I love you.' And, though we have all known the cat who had more than one home, it cannot be considered typical animal-kingdom behaviour. It is unlikely that you will suddenly discover that your cockatoo has another owner down the street, where he keeps a spare perch and cuttlebone, that all the nights he's been telling you he's out exercising at the gym he's actually been flexing his wings with a petite brunette who is into leather. You can't grow apart from a goldfish.

'But look at all the things that a man can do that an animal can't do,' you protest.

And, of course, you have a point. Apart from the obvious, animals can't, for the most part, talk. They can't sing. They can't laugh. (Although a dog will often get the joke, cats, on the whole, have no sense of humour, especially when the joke is on them – in which way they have something in common with most men.) They can't carry the heavy bags or climb up on the roof to see what's making that flapping sound. They can't be sent out on errands (from which they return, two hours later than estimated, with whipping cream instead of soured cream, the wrong size screws, and the letters to be posted still in a coat pocket). They don't normally like to dance. They are, of course, no help at all when there's a clutch of Mormons in blue suits and sincere smiles on the doorstep. But, on the other hand, they rarely wake you at three in the morning because they can't sleep. (Eliza once had a boyfriend who was heavily into analysis and would wake her up at all hours of the night to discuss the dream he'd been having. 'Can you imagine being woken up just as you're about to receive the Pulitzer for photo-journalism by a naked myopic cellist who wants to know if you think that dreaming about the heads of daffodils snapping off in a cold spell is a manifestation of a fear of castration?' Eliza would enquire. None of us could ever imagine it. 'But that's not the worst part,' she'd continue. 'The worst part was that after you'd managed to get your eyes open for a couple of seconds and said, "Yeah, Danny, that's what it sounds like to me. Now why don't you go back to sleep?", he'd wake you up again four minutes later to tell you that he'd been giving it some thought and if he does have a fear of castration it must have something to do with you.')

Nor can pets complain, argue, or tell offensive jokes. Although the piqued cat or hamster will sometimes give you a little nip or scratch to let you know that you're pushing your luck, no one has ever been socked in the jaw by a cockerspaniel who had too much to drink, a bad day at work, or who can't forgive you for flirting with the guy from export sales at the office party. Name me one woman who has lived with her beagle for fourteen years – cooking for him and cleaning for him and making sure that he gets his vitamins and his shots, watching television with him, going for long country walks with him, sleeping with him snoring gently against her back – only to discover in the fifteenth year that he's actually an embezzler or a hired gun or the ruthless rapist the police have been after for the past six years.

'But I get lonely by myself,' you say. 'You can talk to a pet, but they can't talk back. I like to hear the sound of a human voice now and then. The radio always seems to have so much static on it.'

You don't have to be by yourself to feel lonely. Many of the loneliest women I know are in relationships that have been going so long that they can only dimly remember a time when they and their beloved said any more to one another than 'What's for supper?', 'Leftovers from yesterday.' They live together, they shop together, they potter about in the garden together, they go to the cinema together, they go visiting together, they may even sleep together and call each other darling ('Have you seen my acetylene torch anywhere around here, darling?', 'No, darling, it must be where you left it. You know I never touch your things'), but for all practical purposes one of them might as well be living in the Congo and the other on the moon. They speak to each other to elicit information ('where are the car keys?'), to impart information ('I won't be home till late'), to refrain from relaying any information ('well, I'm really knackered, I think I'll go to bed'), to offer constructive criticism, ('you're not going out in that, are you?'). Many couples spend most of their adult lives together, and yet if one were given the anonymous transcript of the other's innermost thoughts they wouldn't be able to identify the thinker.

'That's all very well and good,' you say, 'but I can't sleep at night when I'm on my own, worrying that someone is going to break in. Women are vulnerable.'

All of us, of course, have heard stories of people having unexpected encounters with their local burglars. My friend Samantha eventually married the man she met when he was coming out of her flat with her portable tv and the sandwich toaster in his arms. She wrote to him in prison to tell him that his advice about her stereo had been right, and he wrote back to apologise for trying to steal all her major appliances, and before you knew it they were engaged. Which is not to suggest that even Jane would suggest that getting robbed is a good way to find a prospective bridegroom. Not all uninvited visitors are user friendly. Being men themselves, they tend to be violent, aggressive, and, nine times out of ten, deranged. For this reason, many women feel safer with a man in the house, under the illusion that a man will protect and defend them, and that his very presence will act as a deterrent (rather like keeping a lion chained in the garden to keep the other lions away). It is true, of course, that men show a great deal more respect and fear towards other men than they ever do towards a woman, but in most cases the best recommendation would be to get a dog. For in a situation where a dog will bark like a crazed beast, waking up the neighbours on both sides and charging up and down the garden trying to chew the intruder's foot off, a man will still be sound asleep, mumbling, 'Can't it wait till the morning, honey?' every time you give him a shake, or be debating with you whether or not the sound you heard downstairs was really a burglar or just a figment of your hysterical female imagination, even as the first flickers of torchlight shimmer beneath the door.

If it's affection, loyalty, companionship, trust, devotion and understanding you're looking for, you'd be much better off investing in a couple of food dishes and a litter tray than in six months at Slim-o-club and a lace suspender belt.

7

DIFFICULT MEN

You're laughing, right?

'Ho ho ho,' you're chortling, 'That's like saying dangerous weapons or opportunistic politicians.'

'Ha ha ha,' you're giggling, 'even my sainted grandfather, who devoted his life and his fortune to the cause of world peace, used to throw a wobbly if his three-minute egg was cooked for three-and-a-half.'

Most men, even Jane Fforbes-Smythe would agree, are difficult. They have little fetishes and habits and behaviourisms that are peculiar to their sex. They think (if think they do) very differently from women. While women are busy trying to populate the planet, men are just as busy trying to depopulate it. While women are busy trying to understand their feelings, men are busy trying to deny that they have any. They still don't understand what women want. But just as some chocolate is darker than other chocolate, some men are more difficult than others. The woman interested in establishing a permanent relationship with one in this impermanent world – a relationship that involves a certain amount of closeness and give-and-take – should be aware that some come equipped with more problems than an ocean liner in the desert. And nor am

I speaking here simply of men doing a life sentence in Sing Sing, SAS paratroopers, or political prisoners in the Soviet Bloc. I am speaking here, for instance, of married men, or the recently divorced, or those who are thirty-eight and still living with their parents. I am speaking of men who, no matter how honeyed their voices, sweet their dispositions, gorgeous their smiles, or real their commitment to the ozone layer, present the sort of difficulties that could wear a person down.

Married Men

Many women, women who want a little romance and affection but not the bother of having some guy on a macrobiotic diet sharing their kitchen, prefer married men. Like other people's children, married men are fun to hug and squeeze and make a fuss over on the infrequent occasions when you see them, but it's nice to know that at the end of the visit they go home and give someone else the hard time. Moral (it is unsisterly to sleep with someone else's man) and physical (if she finds out she is within her rights to hurt your body) objections aside, Jane maintains that for the woman who wants no more than a very friendly friend guaranteed to be unreliable, married men are ideal. If nothing else, Jane assures me, they tend to make up in enthusiasm what they lack in time.

'If you're looking for someone who will be there when the cat is dying or water starts pouring through the ceiling,' says Jane, 'then you'd better avoid other people's husbands. But if all you want is a little company and romance they can be just the thing. No ties. No complications. No chance that he's going to ruin a beautiful relationship by moving in.'

That's all fine, as far as it goes, but human beings are funny creatures, as more than one person over the centuries has pointed out. A person says to herself, 'Married man: no commitment, no hassles, no chance of his getting serious when all you want is fun – sounds fine to me', and then she meets this very nice married man who doesn't lead her on or ever once say that his wife doesn't understand him, and she thinks, boomshiva!, this is the one. She tells all her friends that she knows what she is doing, that she is walking into this with her eyes wide open, that she cannot be accused of hurting anyone or wrecking anyone's home. How can his wife be hurt when she doesn't know what's going on? How can his home be wrecked when she isn't even sure where he lives? And then this same person finds herself getting all gooey when he calls her 'Sugar'. She knows he is a busy man with a wife who likes playing backgammon with him in the evenings and children who appreciate it when he shows up at school to hear their recital or watch their play, but she still starts getting pissed off when he cancels a date. She becomes jealous of his wife. 'She has you all the time,' she wails, 'all I want is to spend my birthday with you. Is that too much to ask?' She becomes hysterical when she discovers that all the presents she has given him are locked in the bottom drawer of his desk at work. 'That's all I am to you,' she screams, 'just something to lock away in the bottom drawer.' She forgets that it was she who said, 'There's nothing I hate more than dependency and possessiveness. That's why I'll never get married', and starts talking about all the children she'll never have if she stays in this dead-end relationship. For there are three things to remember when it comes to human behaviour: 1. people thrive on being inconsistent; 2. no one but a nincompoop believes that there is any concrete relationship between theory and practice; 3. logic zips out the window when lust and/or love come dancing through the door. And there are three things to remember when it comes to married men: 1. the chances of him leaving his wife are only slightly better than the chances of saving the rainforests; 2. if he does leave his wife it is highly unlikely that he will wind up with you; 3. if he does wind up with you, you will be his wife, and you already know what she can expect.

A cautionary tale. Several years ago, for no good reason that any of us could see, my friend Jenny fell in love with a man in her office. A married man with four young children. According to Jenny, this man was not only brilliant (a quality she admired) but had a simmering sensuality cleverly camouflaged by the fact that he looked like a hobbit. They began by playing footsie at board meetings. Then they went for chaste, professional lunches in the executive dining room where she chose the wine and he asked her opinions on world affairs. They started going to bars out of town frequented by long-distance lorry drivers and held hands across the table while, on the jukebox Robert Gordon sang 'It's Only Make Believe'. They made out in the car, just like teenagers. 'He makes me feel so young,' she said. 'She makes me feel like a kid again,' he said. Finally, after a number of false starts (one date was cancelled because of his guilt, one date was cancelled because of her guilt, one date was cancelled because his daughter had a severe nosebleed), she invited him over for dinner. She bought two hand-blown champagne glasses and two bottles of Bollinger to mark the occasion. She paid a small fortune for a dress that barely weighed in at half an ounce. He passed out. Soon, of course, they were both madly, passionately, and hopelessly in love. He said that she was the only woman who had ever made him feel really alive. He said it was as though she'd broken a spell. He could never go back to the tedious, life-sapping existence he had had before. He couldn't continue living a lie. He told his wife. His wife felt as though a spell had been broken, as well. She reminded him of their fifteen years together, their children, their plans. She made him go to family counselling with her. Any time she called the office and a woman answered she burst into tears. Jenny was hurt that he seemed to be making more effort to save a marriage he claimed had been dead for fourteen years than to begin a new one. Jenny was hurt because his children wouldn't speak to her. She was upset because although he was always just about to leave his wife something happened to delay him (the youngest had chicken-pox, his wife threatened to kill herself, it was one of the children's birthdays, it was Christmas, it was Easter, it was his birthday, he couldn't find a flat, his wife had given all his clothes away to the Salvation Army). Finally, heartsick, underweight, and having given most of her friends compassion fatigue with her endless unhappiness, Jenny decided to go to Australia for a year or two. While she was away, her lover left his wife and children and moved in with a twenty-year-old designer named Aire. He is now on his third marriage. Jenny has yet to start her first.

The Recently Divorced

As we can deduce from Jenny's story, recently divorced men are likely to be no less complex than men who haven't yet been moved to the couch. The recently divorced man, especially when, as often happens, the divorce was not only not his idea but came as something of a surprise to him ('I had no idea she was so unhappy'), is vulnerable, confused, and generally not quite sure in which direction he's pointing. He will collapse into your arms like a rag doll onto a chair, happy and relieved to find someone who thinks he is attractive and interesting, someone who is sympathetic and supportive, someone who is uncritical and goes out of her way to make his favourite meals, someone, in short, who is not his wife. And you will think, perfect: he's mature, experienced, has made mistakes and learned from them, and he's unattached. Making you wrong on at least three counts (mature is a word normally associated more with cheese than with men; few of us learn any more from our mistakes than to recognize them the next time we make them; and people just coming out of a serious relationship are never unattached). A chain is only as strong as its weakest link, and that includes the chain of love. And when it comes to the chain of love, there is no link weaker than a man who feels rejected and abandoned, a man whose entire life has been turned upside down. He may want a rock on which to pitch his tent, but at the same time he may want to assert his masculinity and prove his desirability by dating every woman he can lay his hands on as well. And, also at the same time, deep within his banged-up heart, where his memories of the first time he kissed his ex-wife and the way they used to talk in squeaky voices during intimate moments when they were first married lie, there may exist the never-to-be-spoken hope that one day (when she can hear his voice on the telephone without immediately slamming the receiver down, for instance) he and his wife may be reconciled. Strength, patience and determination, may, of course, win the day – but strength, patience and determination are not always enough to win a man who feels about his ex-wife's perfume the way he used to feel about his mother's apple crumble.

The other disadvantage that recently (or not-so-recently) divorced men have is that they often have children. Not that I have anything against children as a social group. But if you believe, as many people do, that no relationship comes easily, that they have to be worked at and cared for if they are to develop into something lasting, just like nurturing a plant, then beginning one with a man who has children is the equivalent of trying to grow a lemon tree from seed by planting it out in the snow and stepping on it any time it pokes its little head above ground.

The trouble with children is twofold.

In the first fold we find the child her- or himself. Naturally, most children, especially young ones, tend to be fond of their mothers; much fonder of their mothers than they are going to be of you. Even if Dad were hustled out of the house in the middle of the night at gunpoint by a mum who couldn't stand one more hour of his hoovering the kitchen before he could go to sleep, the child is going to think about her and mum sitting in their lonely, echoing home with the empty place at the table, eating boiled potatoes and catching themselves saying things like, 'Oh, wouldn't Daddy love that?' or 'I wonder if Daddy's watching this programme, you know how fond he is of barn owls', and then think of you and dad always giggling in the hallway and always having pizza and sushi delivered for dinner, and the child is going to blame you. You give the child a present and he tells you his mother already gave him one just like it, but better. You take the child out for the afternoon and she forgets to tell you that she's allergic to bananas and throws up all over tea. You yell at the child for flinging his rice in the air and he tells you to mind your own business, you're not his mother. You spend two days shopping and preparing a meal that will cause his little heart to beat with joy and to feel warmly towards you, and instead of saying, 'Wow, real hickory-smoked hamburgers, homemade chips, roasted corn on the cob and homemade chocolate cake with mint-chip ice cream,' he says, 'Yuk, what's this rubbish? Mummy always makes me nouvelle cuisine.' A child will say things like, 'My mother's not fat like you' or 'What colour is your hair really?'

The child, disturbed by the trauma of divorce, can't sleep when he's staying with his father and is always

wandering into the bedroom in the middle of the night on feet as silent as the feet of ants to sleep with Daddy, something you soon enough stop doing. When a child does get to like you and think of you as a not-so-bad person whose chocolate cake makes up for a multitude of sins, the child will then start treating you the way she treats her mother. She will think nothing of waking you at five in the morning because she suddenly remembered that tomorrow's photograph day for the school band and she doesn't have a clean white blouse. She will use your silk shirt to dry off the dog. She will eat every taco chip in the house.

In the second fold is the child's mother. Every time you look up and find the child staring at you, you know that the child is recording your looks and behaviour for relay back home – you should see what she looks like in the morning, she doesn't even know how to lace up a trainer, she puts mud in her hair, she's always yelling at him. Every time you look up and find the child staring at you, you know that it is really the child's mother eyeing you up and wondering what he could possibly see in you.

My friend Eliza once had a very promising relationship with a recently unwed man, who had left back at home not just his wife, two gerbils and a Russian wolfhound, but one small boy as well. In this case, the boy was not, in fact, any problem. He was sweet, well-behaved, laid-back, and liked everyone except his stepfather. But whenever he came to visit there would be an inventory of his belongings taped to the lid of his suitcase. 'Jimmy has with him the following items: seven pairs of socks, seven pairs of underwear, one heavy blue jumper, three white and two blue T-shirts, one white dress shirt, two flannel shirts, a green and blue rugby shirt, one pair of striped pyjamas, two pairs of jeans and one pair of dress slacks, one dressing gown (new), one pair of sneakers, one pair of heavy shoes, and a maroon sweatshirt. Please check all these things off in the space provided when you are re-packing for him.' When one of his socks went missing, mum was on the phone no more than thirty minutes after Jimmy returned home, wanting to know what had happened to the second navy pair. Also in the suitcase would be a three-page document explaining what Jimmy could and could not eat that week, what his physical and behavioural problems had been recently (for instance, one memorable communique included the information that Jimmy hadn't had a bowel movement for two days so it would be appreciated if Eliza could refrain from giving him too much cheese), and what his mother's analysis of his last visit was (never very good). 'It was like minding children for the Gestapo,' Eliza recalled years later. 'I once spent three hours ransacking the house looking for the seventh pair of underwear – I even rolled up the carpet, though heaven knows how I thought it would have got under there – only to realize forty minutes after he'd missed his train that the seventh pair was the one he was wearing.' Needless to say, fond though she was of both father and son, in the end this sort of pressure proved too much for Eliza.

CBs

Not, as you might have anticipated, certified bastards, but confirmed bachelors. This is an old-fashioned term (and not one that signifies, as my younger sister once believed, that the bachelor in question is Anglican), but so is spinster. Unlike spinster, however, confirmed bachelor has no pejorative connotations. If someone says to you, 'Why don't you come over for dinner on Friday and meet Luke. You must remember me telling you about him. He's the confirmed bachelor with all the sculptures on his lawn,' you don't immediately think to yourself, confirmed bachelor, oh, yuk, he's probably dry and wispy or a close relative of the Wicked Witch of the West, what are these sculptures, garden gnomes? You don't immediately picture some boring old fart who's either a virgin or a homosexual. Someone who saves his fingernail clippings or sleeps on the floor while his fifteen cats sleep in the bed. Of course not. Although the only positive role model for a spinster that one can find is Miss Marple, it is different for confirmed bachelors. You think, wow, confirmed bachelor, like Superman or Sam Spade or Indiana Jones or James Bond. You think, whoopee, this sounds exciting. For it is one of the more fascinating aspects of our culture and language that terms used to describe the same condition in different sexes can have such divergent meanings. So that the term for a man who gets about a good deal is a 'Casanova' or a 'great lover' or 'a stud', and the term for a woman who (presumably) enjoys her carnal pleasures a little more than is considered good for her is a 'slut' or a 'nympho' or a 'whore'. The term for a woman who determinedly looks after herself, getting what she goes after, not letting any person, thing, or passing sentimentality get in her way, is a 'bitch', while a man who exhibits similar characteristics is 'a good businessman'. A woman who leaves her husband and children to go wander around the world having marvellous adventures and memorable experiences is a 'cold-hearted and selfish cow', but a man who gets restless with domestic life and decides to pack his saddlebags and roam is 'a loner'. And thus it is that the term for a woman who has never married suggests that she is one of life's losers, while the term for a man who has never married suggests that he is a person of decision and independence, one of life's winners, a person who has been having his cake and stuffing his face with it too.

In modern usage, the confirmed bachelor breaks down into two distinct types. The first is Indiana Jones. He is attractive (maybe even devastatingly handsome), intelligent, cynical but kind, has a good sense of humour and a great sense of irony, is strong, adventurous, has an interesting job and both muscles and integrity. Women love him, and he loves them – but not for too long. 'Oh,' his sister is wont to sigh to her friends, 'if only Indiana would find the right woman. Sometimes I think he'll never settle down. He'll end up an old man who's never known the joys of family life. But just when he meets some nice girl who really loves him he picks up his whip and goes off courting death, disaster and some other woman again.'

The second type is Milo Bright. Milo lives next door to my mother, with his mother. He is quietly attractive (not the hydrogen bomb of good looks, perhaps, but

kind of cute in a poured custard sort of way),
intelligent enough to be Prime Minister or President of
the United States, strong enough to shift the sofa,
adventurous enough to have gone on holiday to
Greece several times, has a job that is no less
interesting than most, is not Mr Body but has been
heard to sing 'I Did It My Way' in the shower. Women
like Milo – he is courteous and attentive and helpful
and single – and Milo likes them. But though he has,
according to my mother, quite a few women friends,
and though he has, according to his mother, certainly
had a girlfriend or two over the years (though none of
them real Mrs Milo Bright material), and though, when
in his cups on New Year's Eve, he has even been
known to make a racy joke (suggesting that there
might be more to Milo than his polite good mornings
and comments about the dustbin collection have lead
one to believe), Milo has never quite managed to leave
the ancestral semi. 'Oh,' his sister is wont to sigh, 'if
only Milo would find Miss Right. He's such a sweet
guy, and he knows more about sixteenth-century
Venetian politics than anyone else I ever met, and just
look how wonderful he was when Mother had her
operation ... But sometimes I do worry that he'll never
settle down. He'll wind up as one of those old men
who get invited over for Christmas lunch because
everyone feels sorry for him because he's never had a
family of his own. But he never seems to meet anyone
special enough. Every time you think, well, she's nice,
maybe something will happen here, she goes off and
marries someone else and Milo buys her a vase for a
wedding present.'

There is one simple rule concerning confirmed
bachelors of either type. And this is it: if a man has
reached his mid-thirties and never lived with or had a
long-term relationship with a woman (and especially if
he's never left home, university years and a few
overnights with the Boy Scouts not counting), the

chances are that he isn't really interested. There are men who are like that (and, I am happy to be able to say, there are women who are like that too).

'Oh wait a minute, wait a minute,' you say. 'That's not really true. Often, it's just a matter of time. What about Jorge Luis Borges?'

What about him? It is a fact, of course, that Señor Borges lived with his mother (who was eventually a very old woman) all her life, and finally married when he was in his eighties (it was not a long marriage). All I can say to that is that if you marry a man who is eighty (unless, of course, you are also eighty and have been waiting half a century to consummate your up-until-now thwarted love) it isn't too likely that you are marrying for the usual reasons (to have someone around who can deal with the builders, play tennis, and give you an orgasm by blowing in your ear).

'Okay,' you say, 'okay. But what about your friend Alice?'

There are two ways of looking at Alice's story: 1. she is the exception that proves the rule; 2. she lucked out. Alice met Tony two weeks before her fortieth birthday. He was forty-two, had a good job, his own home (although he did not, at the time, have a stove), a steady girlfriend who wanted to marry him, was good to his mother and a nice guy by anybody's standards, a mean bluegrass banjo player, and had no ex-wives lurking in his past. He had never even been engaged. Alice and Tony went out on one date (they met at the tennis club, she somehow having managed to hit him with her ball), which, as she recalls it, was very pleasant, and then he called her two days later to say that though he very much wanted to go out with her again he couldn't at the moment because his aunt had unexpectedly turned up for a visit. Oh sure, Alice thought, his aunt. As it turned out, he did have his aunt staying with him (I told you he's a nice guy), and when she went back to Dublin he called Alice up and they went on a date that lasted two days. That was in July. In August they were married. 'I just don't understand,' Alice said to him later, 'how come you were never married before.' Tony looked surprised. 'But how could I?' he asked. 'I hadn't met you.'

Luck and exceptions aside, confirmed bachelors have something in common with married men. And that is the ability to make you think that one thing is happening (he's leaving his wife, he's about to propose), when actually something quite different is happening (he is not leaving his wife, it has never even occurred to him to propose to you). You go along for years thinking that any week now he's going to suggest that you move in with him, or that the two of you look for a bigger place together, but he never does. When pushed, he always has a good excuse, if not an actual reason. 'Not now,' he says, 'I'm just on my way to Bolivia to find the Holy Grail.' 'Not now,' he says, 'Mother's had a relapse and can't be left on her own.' 'Oh, honey,' he says, 'you know how much I love you. If I ever marry anyone, you're the girl, but I'm not ready for the ring thing yet. I still haven't entirely got Thailand out of my system.' 'Oh, sweetheart,' he says, 'you know how much I care about you, but I wouldn't want to take on the responsibilities of a family until I had a few more sound investments.'

Priests

Like outlaws, priests hold a strange fascination for many women. Women, of course, have no choice but to like a challenge – and what could be more of a challenge (to the imagination as much as to anything else) than a man who renounced his sexuality for ever when he was fourteen? As with the apparently endlessly tantalizing question of what a Scotsman

wears under his kilt, a person can't help but wonder
what sort of heart beats beneath that pristine cassock.

The unattainable, as we all know, is a powerful
aphrodisiac. The man who is sweet and helpful and
always around, willing to drive you into town to do
your Christmas shopping when your car is in for
repairs, willing to mind your cat for the weekend even
when it's not well and can only eat poached cod,
dependable as a Golden Retriever, is, like a Golden
Retriever, unlikely to inspire any great passion. 'Oh,
Harry,' you say to your friends, 'of course I'm fond of
him, he's one of the dearest men in the world, but,
well, you know, I could never take him seriously. I
mean, not like *that*. You know, kissing him would be
about as exciting as kissing your pillow. It'd be like
settling for water when you could have had
champagne.' But put this same man in a black suit
with a dog collar, stick a crucifix in his hand, and call
him Father, and all of a sudden he has the charisma of
Clint Eastwood. Now that you can never have him –
now that there is no chance of his ever cornering you
in the kitchen after he's relaid the floor, and, heady
with the blend of proximity and apoxy, telling you that
though he knows you could never love him the way he
loves you he wants you to know that his feelings for
you will never change, he'll always be there – you start
thinking about him in a way you never would have
before. How big is his penis? Is it true that still waters
run deep? What are his real feelings? Doesn't he ever
long to love a woman? What would it be like to be held
in his arms? Part of the fantasizing that goes on
regarding God's soldiers is not, I suspect, just because
they are unattainable, but might have something to do
with the fact that, historically, they have often been as
attainable as corn in Kansas. It is common knowledge
that priests, like angels, have always had a propensity
for falling, for giving into the temptations of the
flesh (and then tormenting themselves with guilt), for

spreading, along with the Word, the seed. There is, after all, more than one way of looking at the term missionary position.

My advice about priests runs like this. They are all right for the odd fantasy on a chill and cheerless winter night, but for no more than that. Don't start volunteering to arrange the flowers on the altar. Don't start dropping homemade cakes and wines by the rectory. Either you are making a career out of unrequited love, or you are perpetuating on yourself one of the greatest self-delusions since the Indians turned to one another and said, 'Yeah, I think we can get along with these white guys. They seem pretty civilized.' For even if you get beyond the, 'I want to thank you so much, Ms Wishbone, for all your help with the St Patrick's Day Dinner,' level to the 'Ms Wishbone, ever since I met you I have been doubting my vocation,' stage, nine-and-a-half times out of ten you are fighting something that is considerably bigger than both of you. Centuries of tradition and taboo. Decades of belief and practice. A lifetime of conditioning. God. Even if, passion's willing slave, he leaves the church for you and becomes a sheep farmer in Scotland, the time will come when he starts seeing disappointed-looking angels hanging around the hillocks, shaking their heads at him and frowning wistfully. Soon the angels move into the house. Every time he goes to touch you one of them suddenly appears, the expression on its face both mild and disapproving. He starts sleeping on the couch, where he tosses and turns all night, mumbling the Act of Contrition in his sleep. And one day, you're standing at the window, watching him walk towards the house, and you realize that you are looking not at a man of mystery and enchantment, but at a slightly pudgy sheep farmer, and you think to yourself, good old Bob, I wonder what I ever saw in him.

Men in Special Occupations

There are certain jobs whose occupational hazards (or perks) include having women fall in love with you on a regular basis. As a rule, this does not apply to exterminators, insurance salesmen, or car park attendants, but it is, nonetheless, fairly widespread. Film actors. Rock stars. Certain television anchormen. Media personalities. Doctors. Psychiatrists. Teachers. Vets. Lawyers. Dictators. Revolutionaries. Investigative reporters. Criminals. Except for the fact that revolutionaries tend to die young and dictators often have uncertain futures, most of these men present no more problems than your average bus driver or corporate executive. One or two, however, do merit a few words of caution.

Doctors. Doctors are everybody's favourite to fall in love with. (Even gynaecologists, though why anyone would want to share chop suey with a man who knows more about her periods than she does is beyond me.) There you are, ill or injured, afraid, in need of miracles, in need of sober, compassionate advice or a knowledgeable, no-nonsense 'Don't get yourself so worked up, Ms Wishbone, just use this cream for a day or two and you'll be as good as new' – and there he is. Calm, professional, reassuring, ready to stop the pain or mend the arm or bring you through the operation with a kindly smile and a charming joke about hospital food. It is a short step indeed from gratitude to ardour. One minute you're thanking him for such tiny stitches, and the next minute you're thinking about licking his knuckles. A person should keep in mind, however, that while she is gazing at her doctor with a heart beginning to go pfft pfft with lust and longing, he is looking at her and seeing a blocked nasal passage or a tilted womb. It can be a very big move from 'Put the drops in your eyes three times a day and come back in a week if the infection doesn't clear up', to 'Ms Wishbone, today as I was operating on someone's ingrown toenails I had a sudden image of you and wondered if you'd like to go dancing one night.' For one thing, one rarely sees one's doctor when one is at one's best. Visits are usually short. If you are in the hospital because you threw your back out lifting weights, you might see your doctor every day, but you're not going to be in any condition to do anything about it.

Jane's solution to this, the time she had a crush on the new doctor in the practice, was to develop a string of minor ailments. On Monday it was an earache. On Wednesday she thought she might have cracked a rib. On Friday she was feeling faint. The next Monday it was recurring headaches. Each time she went into the surgery, she spent several hours beforehand getting ready so that instead of looking like 'another sick person' she would look terrific. It seemed to be working quite well for a while. The receptionist became a little sniffy, 'Oh, it's you again. What is it this time?', but young doctor Farrell showed her nothing but sympathy.

'You certainly do seem to be getting everything that's going at the moment,' he said.

'Not quite everything,' breathed Jane.

'Are you working too hard?' he wanted to know. 'Perhaps you're run down.'

And then, as luck would have it, Jane had an accident. She was run down – by a skateboarder while she was taking out the rubbish. Despite her protests that she had to change and fix her hair before she could go to the doctor, her next-door neighbour bundled her into her car and delivered her to the surgery without even giving her time to put on make-up. 'He didn't even recognize me,' said Jane. 'And how could he? There I was in my old jeans and a sweatshirt with bleach spots on it, looking pale and frumpy and with my foot turning blue. He thought I was just another sick person. I never had the heart to go back.'

Teachers. Teachers are used to having their female students fall in love with them, and, if one can believe all one hears and reads, equally used to falling in love with their female students. In secondary school a crush on your teacher means that you always do his homework, you hang around after class to ask him questions, you never bunk his lesson, and that he always mentions his girlfriend when you walk him to his car so that you can continue your discussion on the endocrine system. Later, however, a crush on your teacher has a chance to develop into something more serious.

Teacher-student affairs are difficult to begin and harder to maintain. So, all right, you sign up for Sociology 1 at the adult education centre because the man who teaches it looks like William Hurt. So then what? You come to class looking as seductive as possible, you sit in the front row so he gets a whiff of your perfume every time he passes your desk, and you make sure you're prepared for every lesson so you can raise your hand a lot. Yet when you linger after class so that you and he just happen to be walking down the same hallway at the same time, he doesn't turn to you and say, 'Ms Wishbone, would you like to have a cup of coffee with me? I think we have some things to discuss', but, 'Ms Wishbone, are you sure you understood the chapter on deviant behaviour?' If something does develop, then the real troubles begin (especially if complicated by the fact, as it sometimes is, that there is a wife at home, keeping the kids out of his study and keeping an eye on his cholesterol intake). Since no one, except for your six best friends and his old girlfriend, is meant to know what's going on, you are constantly under pressure to pretend that nothing is. This means that if you and he had an argument the night before about your sister, when you get to class in the morning you have to act as though you didn't call him a pompous dickhead and make him sleep in the bath. When you answer a question and he smiles sarcastically and says, 'I don't think, Ms Wishbone, that that is what Karl Marx meant by surplus value,' you can't snap back, 'Take your surplus value and stuff it in your ear. How can a man who can't sew a button on his shirt teach anybody else anything?' And when you are speaking to one another, it entails a lot of polite nods in the corridor and quick gropes in cars parked up deserted cul-de-sacs; it means sneaking about and dissembling all the time. Dating one of your teachers is a lot like being a friend of Michael Jackson's: not only is it a constant strain, but you can't tell anyone about it. And people do sometimes get restless when they can't bore all their friends rigid with stories of their love – 'Did I ever tell you about the cute way he always wears an orange knitted hat when he's cooking?', 'Did you know he spent ten days in Montana?' 'Did I show you that picture of him after he fell into the lake?' 'Did you know he once had a letter published in *The Times*?' You can't very well go up to one of your classmates in the library one day and say, 'Did I ever tell you about the time Mr Taylor and I were making love and the bed broke?'

Nor should a person assume that just because a man is in love with her during the autumn term that he will still be in love with her after the Christmas break. Nor should a person assume that just because a man is reinforcing his lecture on Cavalier poetry with a little swordplay of his own that he is going to be any less withering to her than to his other students, any less likely to smile with just his thin lips and say, 'Blake, Ms Wishbone? What makes you think you're capable of understanding Blake?' What a person can assume is that on the Tuesday night before your final exam, when you have tickets to see U2, he's going to tell you that you can't afford not to stay home and study, and he'll go with someone else.

Outlaws. Long before Robin first scaled the castle wall to save Maid Marion, ladies have been falling in love with outlaws. There is nothing like fooling around with a man who may be dangerous to make a person's skin glow. There is nothing like throwing in your lot with a man who is totally unsuitable – a man who is not only not approved of by your mother, your aunts, the woman who runs the local launderette and all your friends, but a man of whom the Queen herself would take a dim view – to bring out a person's fire and spirit. If love is the stew, danger, excitement, and looming doom are the spices.

In legend, men like Dick Turpin and Jesse James and even (rather inexplicably) Billy the Kid are figures of romance and yearning. In films and novels men like these have either been maligned by a hostile establishment or turn out to be somebody else (an undercover agent, a prince in exile, the real hero); somebody worth having. In real life, however, in this as in many other things, the truth is rarely as much fun as the make-believe. Outlaws have their in-built problems. They have to move a lot. They don't always turn up for dinner when they promised. They can't get a mortgage (unless, of course, we're talking about stock brokers and members of the government).

I was once visiting a very good friend of mine while he was in prison. 'Hey,' I said, after the preliminaries were over, 'I met this guy on the way in who says he knows you. He seemed like a very nice guy.' 'Serena,' said my friend, with a new-found patience, 'none of us are in here for being nice guys.' The answer to that, of course, is that none of us are out here for being nice guys either – but there is something worth thinking about in his admonishment.

A man who is on the run because he was framed by corrupt CIA agents trying to keep him from telling the world the truth is obviously a man of commitment, integrity and ideals. You, who loved Zorro and applauded his one-man war against the authorities, find this powerfully attractive. Oh ho ho, you think, this is the alienated hero of my dreams. This is a man whose fight I want to share. I can see the two of us now, barely breathing as we hide in the rat-infested loft, while below us the enemies of Good scour the barn for us, machine guns cocked. 'Don't worry, darling,' his eyes tell me, 'I'm not going to let them win.' You recognize the same electricity that flowed between Harrison Ford and Kelly McGillis in *Witness* flowing between you and Leonard. What you've forgotten is that Harrison Ford and Kelly McGillis had their afternoon of unbearably beautiful passion and then he went back to the city and she settled down with the farmer. What you've forgotten is that Zorro didn't have a girlfriend. Zorro never had to mow the lawn or help with the cooking or worry that he was going to cause some upset if he returned home at two in the morning dripping blood. Jesse James did not go to your friend Fiona's for dinner and start an argument about the safety of nuclear waste. Superman may turn up at crucial moments when Lois Lane really really needs him, but he is not a man to make a soufflé for. Billy the Kid was a psychopath.

I once had a serious relationship with an absolutely wonderful man who was sort of lying low from one or two different groups of people. Except for the fact that he had to work the night shift in a light fittings factory, and thus was not around during those moments when a person was tired of watching television and was looking for something else to do, this man was perfect. If men were stones, he would have been a diamond to everyone else's quartz. He had a great sense of humour, he was smart, he could breakdance, he made the best blue corn tortillas east of New Mexico, he was a wonderful and considerate lover, and his all-time favourite movie was *His Girl Friday*.

What went wrong?

It is difficult to settle down into a comfortable lifestyle (even an exciting comfortable lifestyle) when every time the phone rings you expect it to be the police or the hospital, when every time there is a knock on the door you expect some guy who looks like he was an adviser in the Reagan administration to walk in. At first you think that there is nothing more romantic in the cosmos than you and Watford's answer to Ché Guevara, alone against the world, on the side of justice. You picture yourself as Princess Leah in *Starwars*, shoulder to shoulder with your man (or in her case, men). But in real life you don't get a laser gun, let alone a speaking part. He says, 'This is no life for you, Ms Wishbone,' and you say, 'Oh, yes it is. I don't mind not having any friends. I don't mind worrying about you every minute of the day. I don't mind not having a credit rating. I don't mind never seeing my family. So what if I couldn't go to my sister's wedding? She'll probably get married again sooner or later. It doesn't bother me that I had to change my name. I don't care that I am destroying my hair with chemical dyes and can never go to brightly lit public places. I enjoy being creative with lentils and left-overs. All that matters is that we're together.' But as the days sneak on, you both begin to wonder if you're lying. You begin to get on each other's nerves. Every time he starts banging on about the corrupt establishment and how it is up to the individual to protect her/his own freedoms, you imagine being able to go to Sloppy Charley's with all your old friends for stuffed chillis and sangria. You try to recall what it was like to go over to someone's house for an evening without being terrified that a friend of theirs was going to walk in, take one look at your boyfriend, and say, 'Hey, you look familiar. Don't I know you from somewhere?' He accuses you of being just like your parents.

Outlaws are wonderful for the two-week-affair-of-a-lifetime. The sort of affair that, years later, when you're an old lady, rocking away by the fire with the cat on your lap, you will remember with an enigmatic smile that drives your grandchildren nuts. But if you want someone for forty years of upward-mobility, PTA meetings, camping holidays, pleasant family evenings and a BMW, stick to the estate agent.

Spies. It hardly needs saying, but of all the prospective partners a person might consider, spies are definitely one of the trickiest. If you're the sort of person who thinks that the best relationships are ones where the woman is in one country and the man in the other, then a spy might prove a perfect mate. Otherwise, though, spies not only tend to spend a lot of time away from home, missing holidays and children's birthdays and every anniversary, but they are dangerous to know. It's all very well and good for him to get a thrill out of shooting it out with the bad guys while hanging from a hovering helicopter, but spies have a way of involving their loved one in their adventures as well. They want to get him, so they kidnap you. They want him to stop what he's doing, so they tie you to a chair in an abandoned warehouse. Because of the nature of their job – the alienation and isolation, the loneliness of badly lit Eastern European hotel rooms, the steamy cafes where the distinctive aroma of boiled cabbage and chicken clings to the walls, the constant danger and insecurity – spies are always seeking a few hours of comfort in the arms of beautiful and innocent daughters of imprisoned dissidents and scientists on the verge of defecting. So, to be practical, what do you get in the end? You get a man who is never home; who when he is home is pretending to be someone he isn't; who when he isn't home is either being ambushed as he strolls along a crowded street, hanging off a building while some thug jumps on his fingers, or making love to some gorgeous woman who shakes his martinis between her breasts. Since the odds are against him living long enough to retire, you have nothing to look forward to unless you look really stunning in black.

Heads of State. Oh sure, you pick up the morning paper, and there is Mrs Bush, or Mrs Gorbachev, or Denis Thatcher, looking attractive and happy in an expensive suit with a bodyguard looming behind one shoulder, and you think to yourself, hey, that wouldn't be a bad way to live. You're expected to spend (or, not spend) a fortune on clothes. You get to invite rock stars and film actors to dinner. You're seen as a nice person because you're always being photographed with orphans and cripples and refugees. You drink a lot of champagne because you're always opening hospitals and libraries and crematoriums and missile plants. You have servants. Your husband is nearby, but not so nearby that he gets under your feet. You can have tea with the Queen. Yeah, well. Being the spouse of a head of state looks like a good deal (and it is certainly a lot more glamorous than being the spouse of someone who puts the hubcaps on the cars at the Ford plant), but, like steer riding, it isn't half as much fun as it looks. You travel a lot, but you never get to see anything except hospitals, schools, singing children, marching soldiers, and the occasional war memorial or statue. You have an expensive wardrobe, but it rarely consists of much that a real person, whose greatest repeating nightmare is waking up to discover that she looks like a friend of Nancy Reagan, would want to wear.

In addition, though Mr Gorbachev certainly seems

like a sweetie, most heads of state tend to be a little on the boring and pompous side. Accustomed to standing at podiums and droning on for hours while the newspaper reporters (who already have a transcript of the speech on their laps) think about the novels they're going to write and everyone else slips into a state of semi-coma, they often take this style of relating home with them. You say, 'Gee, honey, what are we going to do about the woodworm in that old desk in the study?' and he launches into a forty-five minute talk on an ounce of prevention being worth a pound of cure, and how there are always several options open to the intelligent person, freedom is the most important thing we have and something we must fight for, and there is a lot about wood in the Bible. Accustomed to keeping his firm and decisive answers noncommital, he sometimes finds it a hard habit to break. You say, 'Honey, would you like ham or chicken for dinner on Sunday?' and he says that ham is good, and chicken is good, though, naturally, too much of either is bad, and of course he, like all right-thinking people, would want to be assured that the hams and chickens were being treated humanely, though, sadly, it isn't always possible, but that, of course, is no one's fault, and he would be delighted to have ham for dinner on Sunday and also pretty thrilled to have chicken.

Artists. Painters, musicians, poets, sculptors, potters and prose stylists, though they can look pretty impressive on a person's social cv ('I see here, Ms Wishbone, that you have dated one abstract expressionist, two pianists, three poets, and one fantasy writer, and that you once shared a cab with Mark Knopfler. That's very interesting, very interesting indeed. You are obviously not as shallow and frivolous as your shocking-pink tights and sequined tank top would lead one to believe'), all share one common flaw. They take themselves very seriously. Whether they're writing prose that redefines the modern novel or lyrics for Bananarama, whether they're painting wall-size murals of destroyers or miniatures of kittens on shells, they all think that what they're doing is more important than what everyone else is doing. Okay, so doctors do contribute something to the world's well-being, and farmers and firemen are pretty necessary, but doctors, firemen and farmers are concerned only with the body, while artists, of course, are concerned with the soul. Artists are special. Artists transcend the mundane.

'It sounds all right to me,' you say. 'If a person doesn't take himself seriously, who will? Look at it like that.'

And that, of course, is true. And it is also true that due to the largely reclusive nature of their occupations it is only natural that creative types should become a little self-obsessed. If you've spent ten hours painting a sky or practicing that tricky Mozart concerto or searching for something to rhyme with eurystomatous or singing 'Gloria', it is unlikely that at the end of the day you're going to emerge from your workroom and want to start discussing rising interest rates or Mona Henderson's dentures.

But it is not, I would think, too much to expect that after an hour or so, when the real world (where a painting is just a picture and a poem is just that little bit less important than the latest Prince single and Mozart is just another dead composer) has had a chance to assert itself, he will be able to shift his attention to something other than himself. Artists, however, often have a great deal of trouble in doing this. They are interested in other people only as far as they relate to them (as in, 'does she admire my work?'). They expect everyone else to be interested in them. They are interested in outside events only as they relate to them. In other homes, guests are expected to admire the new carpet or the Victorian toy collection or the children; in the home of the artist, guests are expected to sit gazing at the representation of four pink frogs floating through a green and yellow sky for ten solemn minutes, and not to say anything gauche like, 'Is this supposed to mean something?' or 'I always like what's-his-name's work, you know, the man who's always painting swimming pools'. Novelists normally refrain from carrying their manuscripts around with them and so are confined to entertaining their friends with the plot synopsis of the four-book, 500,000-word epic on ancient Malaya that they're writing over the wine and salted chickpeas (and well into the coffee and Turkish Delight), but poets have no such constrictions. Poets will turn up at anything from a wedding to a funeral with the history of the world in iambic pentameter clutched under one arm, and in the first lull in the conversation (while the bride is cutting the cake, for instance) will say with all the grace of the Queen getting ready to hand out the Christmas presents at the children's ward, 'Would you like me to read the poem I'm working on?', already into the dedication before anyone can say no.

There is a time in a woman's life, usually around the age of twelve or so, when she likes to imagine what it would be like to be married to a famous poet or painter or (to be a little more modern) brooding rock star. She imagines it would be pretty wonderful. All those parties. All that attention. People always coming up to you and saying, 'Oh, you're so lucky', and 'Is that poem about the dying otter about you?', and 'You were the model for the portrait of Joan of Arc, weren't you?' and 'I hear he named one of his guitars after you.' She imagines it will be the same as being an artist herself, but with none of the work.

Don't kid yourself. Think of Mrs Picasso. For the person involved with an artist, life is hard and not always kind. You will be expected to give solace, support, critical opinion (though, of course, if your opinion is that the perspective is a little off or the images in the greyhound poem seem hackneyed, you are nothing more than an untrained idiot with the soul of a treacle tart), encouragement, love, and from time to time, inspiration. (You needn't get too excited about this inspiration lark. Cast any illusions of becoming the New Age Mona Lisa or Dark Lady permanently aside. It is much more likely that what you will inspire is a quick sketch of a woman in a temper, a poem entitled 'Mary in the kitchen lights the stove', or the catchy refrain, 'her toes are cold, her toes are cold, she's pretty to look at, but her toes are cold'.) You will be expected to sit up all night to finish reading the novel, even if he's gone out partying with his friends or you have to get up at dawn to get ready for your address to the United Nations ('Of course I'm not saying you have to read it right now,' he says, putting it carefully down on the bed just on top of your crinkle-crepe playsuit. 'You're an adult, Ms Wishbone, I don't think you need me to explain what your priorities should be.').

This is a long story, and one that probably belongs in another book, but I was once held prisoner in a Tuscan farmhouse for five days by a writer of psychological thrillers, who had been sent into exile so that he would finish his novel, surrounded by Italians, with whom he did not share a common language and by whom, therefore, he couldn't be distracted. Six months of linguistic isolation, however, unhinged Albert to such an extent that I only escaped by sneaking out the bathroom window in the middle of the night and hitching a ride on a chicken truck.

And who do you think it is answers the artist's telephone, feeds his admirers, makes sure his bills are paid, locates his glasses and his favourite brush? Who nurses him through his writer's block or the trouble with the record company? And don't think that, in turn, he will be interested in domestic crises or the problems of you and your friends (unless, that is, they might make a good short story). He will wake you up at inconvenient hours to read you a line or get your impression of how the trees are coming along. But you will come home from work after a day that tried to kill you, your head aching and your body exhausted, wanting no more than a hot bath and a cold wine, and walk into the living room to find it filled with poets arguing about Ted Hughes and wondering when supper's going to be served.

Your friends, when they learn that you are dating an artist, will say things like, 'Oh, a composer/sculptor/poet/drummer – he must be so sensitive.' And that is true, of course, he is sensitive. Sensitive to a change in light or mood or sound when the muse is upon him, and at all other times sensitive to himself. In arguments over which of you is to take off half a day to talk with the roofer or chaperone his mother on her visit to the chiropodist, you never win because your time, not being spent in transcending the mundane, is negligible. In arguments over who understood what the film meant or what was going on between Clive and Olivia at the party or why you threw the bowl of prawn crackers at him when all he'd done was ask a civil question, you will always lose because you are a woman who wears magenta nail polish and he is a genius.

Men at Work. Any person who has ever seen *The Apartment* shouldn't need to be told about the dangers of becoming involved with men at work.

Lovers are disruptive to the smooth running of the workplace. They keep disappearing into empty rooms and fire exits. Other workers become wary of entering a room suddenly, especially if it is early in the morning or late in the evening, because of the high risk of coming upon two people who normally refer to each other as 'Miss Marshall' and 'Mr Firmbank' going at it like rabbits under the boardroom table. It is hard to concentrate on what he is saying about the number of wing-bolts used in Saudi Arabia per annum when you are reflecting on the way he always cries out 'Oh, baby, oh,' whenever you bite his shoulder.

One of the few interesting things about office affairs is that no matter how discreet and clever you think you are, everyone else in the office, if not the entire building, will know what's going on approximately four hours before you do. They will know when you meet. They will know at every step what stage the relationship is at. 'They went away for the weekend,' Sandra will tell Inez as they remove the covers from their computers on Monday morning. 'Where to?' asks Inez. 'His brother's place at the seaside.' 'How do you know?' asks Inez. 'I heard him on the phone on Friday and when he came in this morning there was seaweed stuck to his shoe.' 'Wow,' says Inez. 'They're sure moving fast. I wonder what it was like ...' Sandra rolls her eyes. 'Oohwee,' says Sandra. 'You should see him. He looks like Don Johnson on a roll. I bet he hasn't slept or shaved since Friday morning. "Oh, Mr Smothers," I said to him. "You look like you've been working too hard again." ' 'And what did he say?' asks Inez. 'He said, "I know, Sandra, but somebody's got to do it." ' Inez and Sandra both start laughing rather uncontrollably here. 'And what about Ms Wishbone?' asks Inez once she's recovered. 'I haven't seen her yet this morning.' Sandra can barely answer, she's laughing so hard. 'Oh her,' chokes Sandra, 'she called in sick.' Inez nearly falls off her chair.

They will not only know every time you and your lover have an orgasm, they will know every time you have a fight. 'Stay away from the two of them today,' Inez will warn Sandra. 'Why?' asks Sandra, glancing up from her terminal. 'What's up?' 'Not him,' says Inez. 'They had a real knock-down-drag-out because he went out drinking with the boys last night and forgot he had a date with her.'

They will know long before you do when the relationship is coming to an end. 'Did you see that?' Sandra asks Inez one Friday night as the hands of the clock are skipping towards five-thirty. 'Am I blind?' Inez wants to know. 'I haven't seen him move so fast since he set fire to his waste basket that time.' Just then you come by, looking as though you have one or two little things you have to finish up before you go home for the weekend, and looking as though it only occurred to you a few minutes ago that if Mr Smothers hasn't gone home yet he might be able to answer one or two of your questions. 'He's gone,' says Sandra as you come to an abrupt halt at the entrance to Mr Smothers' office, noticing, not for the first time, just how much its neatness, its white walls and chrome fixtures reminds you of his bathroom at home. 'Gone home?' you say, as though it is impossible to understand how a man who has not 'gone home' on a Friday evening for the past six months but has lingered in the office until everyone else had left so that you and he could do some heavy breathing against the filing cabinets could possibly have changed his habits. 'Yes,' says Inez, exchanging with Sandra a look that is not without its sisterly compassion. 'Gone home.'

Older Men. 'Men my own age are so immature,' you say. 'I want someone who knows what life's about. An older man will not only appreciate my great character, charming personality, and scintillating intelligence, he will be grateful for my other qualities as well. My still-firm body, my smooth skin, my extensive training in classical ballet. He will not just be proud to be seen with me, he'll be thanking his lucky stars. This is not a man who is going to take up the best years of my life and then leave me for a cheerleader named Lilac.'

'I know what you're going to say,' you say. 'You're going to say that I'm looking for a father figure.'

Actually, I wasn't going to say that. Even if you

were, it doesn't seem to me that looking for a father figure is any more bizarre than looking for someone who is just like you but has a penis, or looking for Zorro. What I was going to say was that everything you said makes sense. It's all very reasonable. The only fault that I can find with your arguments is that the description above doesn't actually fit most older men.

Huh?

From what one can gather from television and films, older men who have lost everything – their brilliant careers, their families, their mansions on the hill, their stocks and bonds and foreign bank accounts; who have become victims of alcohol and now live on the streets in cardboard boxes, eating in soup kitchens and scrounging enough money for a drink now and then – attain a state of wisdom and understanding most usually associated with Buddhist monks. But they are the only ones. In all other cases, the only difference between a younger man and an older man is that the former hasn't gone bald yet and the latter is likely to have paid off his mortgage.

'Oh come on,' you say. 'I can't believe that. You mean to tell me that a man who is, let's say, sharing living space with fifty years, who has, probably, had a wife and family and has a solid career and knows pretty much just who he is and what he can expect, that a man like that isn't the ideal mate?'

I am amazed, of course, that you can still think in terms of ideal mates, but, yes, that is what I mean to tell you. Let's look at this logically for a minute. Where do older men come from? Of course, they come from younger men. And how do they get from y to o? They get there through relationships with a series of women, from mothers and sisters to girlfriends and wives, all of whom pick up after them, worry about them, and make sure they have cake for their birthday and their favourite meal when they're feeling down. If a man can't cut himself a slice of bread or boil an egg when he is twenty he is not going to be able to do it when he's fifty, and he's going to be even less likely to think that he should. If a man is a demanding, egotistical and selfish jerk when he is twenty-five the chances are that at fifty-five he will be just as demanding, egotistical, selfish and jerkish, only he will be more adept at disguising it as charm and wisdom after all those years of practice. For the years that bring brittle hair, bad teeth, loss of eyesight, varicose veins, and an aversion to overly spicy foods, do not, as a matter of course, bring sagacity and cosmic understanding. Or, as my grandmother once put it, the child is not only father to the man, he is his constant companion.

If the older man you're thinking of is Paul Newman, this weakness on your part is at least perfectly understandable. If it isn't Paul Newman, you should give it a lot of thought before you do something silly.

Younger Men. Younger men have been enjoying a recent surge of popularity. Women who had always believed what they were told – that it is unseemly for a fantastic woman of thirty-five to be seen with a handsome young man of twenty, that he is only interested in her for her money or because she makes apple pie just like his mother, but perfectly natural for a reasonable man of thirty-five to date a stunning young woman of nineteen – are beginning to suspect that they've been handed another apple. They look at the men their own age and instead of thinking, hey, he's cute, as once they would have, they find themselves thinking, well, I guess he's all right. They discover that in men their own age, it is not just the body, the hair, and the determination to sail around the world on a raft that has gone, but the fire as well. 'Harry's a nice guy and everything,' they say, 'but, well, I know this is going to sound strange, but he's so old. He doesn't want to go out dancing. He doesn't want to take up windsurfing. He thinks that what you do on a beach is watch the young women tanning. We may be the same age, but he looks like my father. I don't want to sit around reading *My Twenty-Five Years with General Motors*, I want to have some fun.'

What younger men have in their favour is youth, energy, enthusiasm, freshness, stamina and an optimistic attitude towards life (they aren't worried that they're going to have a heart attack if they eat more than one egg a week). This does not, however, make them perfect. For what they have against them is the fact that they tend to date women their own age and that they don't know any of your favourite songs.

Real Bad News Men. This category shouldn't really need any discussion, but women are no less strange than men at times. Even an intelligent and experienced woman who has seen it all before and knows the score can meet a man who has 'I am real bad news' written all over him, and instead of turning sharply on her heel and rushing off to the next room to get back into the conversation on Israel, she says, 'I don't believe we've met before. My name's Ms Wishbone.' Six years later, still bruised and scarred, having finally moved to a tent in the desert, a place where she is sure he will never find her, never come around drunk out of his brain at three in the morning, throwing things at the window and yelling for her to come down and see what he's got for her, she can only think to herself, was I crazy? Why did I spend so much time on that creep?, questions to which the desert wind does not have an answer, and nor does anyone else.

Real bad news men are not men who pose problems or come with extra sets of difficulties; they are men who should be avoided at all costs, from the word go. Don't even stop to check the colour of his eyes. Don't pause to wonder what size his neck is. Don't think to yourself, okay, he's got a little problem with alcohol, but I'm sure that'll pass once he's happy and secure with me. Don't say to yourself, well, heck, everybody gets depressed once in a while, I mean, who wouldn't? He'll be fine once we move in together and he feels really loved. 'Oh hey,' you tell your best friend, 'he did have this little drug problem a few years back, but he's fine now.' 'Yeah, I know,' you say to your sister, 'I heard that he was a little violent, too. But that was with other women. I'm sure they drove him to it. Really. He's such a nice, gentle guy. He loves me. I know he wouldn't hurt me for anything. We talked about it and that's what he said.'

It is yet another interesting aspect of human behaviour that each of us believes that we are so different and special that we can change, if not the course of rivers, the course of someone's character, personality and actions. We think that if somebody says he loves us that he will act accordingly. This is not true. A man who is real bad news – who isn't just going through a rough patch, who doesn't just have his little oddnesses like everybody else – is not going to be changed because he has someone to sleep with every night and make him soup. Life is hard enough without making sure that you stay in the rocks.

'Hey, wait a minute!' I hear you cry. 'If married men are out, and divorced men are tricky, and priests and confirmed bachelors and outlaws pose serious problems, and men at work, artists, older men and younger men are all pretty iffy, and men with behaviour disorders and addictive tendencies shouldn't even be spoken to, who is there left?

Bruce Springsteen.

Even I realize, however, that we cannot all date Bruce Springsteen. He not only already has a wife and girlfriend, but he spends quite a lot of time with his band. So, obviously, if a person is ever to leave her house after eight o'clock on a Saturday night for any

other reason than to get the Sunday papers or a carton of milk for the morning she is going to have to be able to judge between insurmountable difficulties and limited liabilities. Here we go.

The How Can You Tell if He's Worth a Shot? Quiz

Select the answer that best describes the situation and person to whom you would respond most positively.

1. You go into the sandwich bar near the office for a quick cup of soup and one of their famous humus

sandwiches on wholemeal bread, when who should sit down next to you but this really nice looking doctor from the hospital across the street. You have seen him in here before, and once you even accepted his opinion on the cream cheese and olives on rye. Today he says, 'Is anybody sitting here?' with an especially charming smile, and when he notices that you both have identical lunches makes a little joke about great minds working in a similar way. As you sip your soup and try to eat your sandwich without dropping half of it into your lap, the two of you chat about this and that. During the course of this conversation he discovers that you are gainfully employed and neither married nor engaged, and you discover that he and his wife have been separated for the past six months, you know how it is, just one of those things. 'Oh yes,' you say, 'I know.' You then go on to tell him how traumatic you found your break-up from your boyfriend of nearly six years. 'Even when it's perfectly amicable and you're still good friends and everything, it takes a lot out of you,' you say. 'Henry used to collect stamps, you know. It was two years after he moved out before I could pick up the post in the morning without bursting into tears.' He says,

a. 'I know exactly what you mean. My mother's always trying to set me up with women from her aerobics class, but I really don't feel that I'm ready for any sort of relationship yet. When I get home from work I still have to stop myself from calling out, "Honey, I'm home!" '

b. brushing his arm against yours as he reaches for his tea, 'And just how do you feel about the postal service now?'

c. 'At least I'm thankful that I don't feel angry. I've come to terms with the situation and I can see now that we simply grew apart. At least now we each have an opportunity to find our real selves. Would you like another orange juice?'

2. Will (who is a painter) and Wanda (who is a writer) have a Halloween party, to which everyone must come, of course, in fancy dress. Will and Wanda, unlike most of us, give really good parties, largely because they have a big house, lots of uninhibited, fun-loving friends, and a great record collection. Because you have been to a Will and Wanda party before and know that most of their friends are artistic types with heavy-duty egos and strong sex drives, you decide to go as something unprovocative: a cup of cocoa. You strike up a conversation over the blue cheese dip with a very attractive man masquerading as a priest. He loves your costume. You love his smile. He's amazed that you like Smokey Robinson as much as he does. You're astounded that he is as concerned about man's destruction of his environment as you are. It's incredible that you both would rather eat mashed potatoes with gravy and a side order of onion rings than almost anything else in the world. You win him over completely when you become the first cup of cocoa he has ever seen boogie on down. During a break in the music, you ask him what he does when he's not eating bits of cauliflower stuck in a diseased cheese and dressing as a priest. He

a. says, 'It's funny you ask that, because I almost always dress as a priest. I'm Wanda's brother, Father Burns. Hasn't she told you about me? She's certainly told me about you, but you're even nicer than she said.'

b. says, 'Well, actually, up until about eight months ago I always dressed as a priest, but I found that I was no longer sure that I didn't want a home and family – I couldn't reconcile my feelings as a man with my beliefs as a priest. Now I teach underprivileged children in the inner city and am looking for a serious relationship with the right cup of cocoa.'

c. chokes on his carrot stick. When you have saved his life by slamming him in the chest and he has recovered sufficiently to thank you, he says, 'Actually, I am a priest. I'm an old friend of Will's. I suppose I could have come as a dustbin or something like that, but then no cute cups of cocoa would have wanted to talk to me. Can I get you some more wine, Ms Wishbone, to thank you again for saving my life?'

3. You're still at Will and Wanda's party, but by now you've decided that maybe a cup of cocoa is a little too unprovocative, so you've ditched the cup (papier mâché) and the marshmallows (foam) in the room with the coats and are mingling in your brown leggings and the old brown terry-cloth robe the cat gave birth to her kittens on (it isn't easy to find things that can pass for hot chocolate). A man dressed as, one assumes, himself in a plaid flannel shirt, baggy black trousers and his hair in a pony tail, the tell-tale aroma of turpentine competing with his undeniably sexy aftershave, asks if you're meant to be an in-patient. You laugh, ha ha. You ask him if he's meant to be the lead singer of U2. He

a. is caught with a taco chip laden with guacamole in his hand and a helpless case of giggles. 'I wish I'd thought of it,' he gasps at last.

b. says, with all the humour of a Russian customs guard, 'I couldn't think of anything I'd rather come as than myself.' When you greet this piece of valuable information with a movement towards the pizza crackers, he adds, 'I'm an artist.'

c. says, 'Who?'

4. Your sister, who is worried that you're going to end up an old maid with no one to care for you and a meagre pension, like Aunt Alicia, invites you to the theatre with her, her husband, and one of his business associates, a fabulously wealthy and handsome man in his early forties who drives a silver Ferrari and owns several houses, scattered around the world. As rarely happens when your sister builds someone up to you, this man exceeds your expectations. He is handsome, charming, sophisticated, amusing, thoughtful, considerate, intelligent, treats even the usher who drops the torch on his foot as though he's a person, and insists on taking everyone to dinner. Your sister and brother-in-law have to get home for the sitter, leaving you two alone in a nearly empty restaurant, talking intensely in the flickering candlelight. After the third brandy, you say, 'You know what I can't understand, Raoul?' He says, 'No, my dear Ms Wishbone. What is it you can't understand?' 'I can't understand why you never wed.' He

a. says, 'I can't either.'

b. looks sadly and wistfully at his elegant hands, on which the gold rings sparkle forlornly in the romantic lighting. 'Ah,' he sighs. 'It isn't easy building up a billion-dollar business out of nothing. It's taken all my attention and energy. Somehow there hasn't been time for love ... time for a family ...' he plucks a single velvety petal from the white rose on the table '... it's incredibly lonely at the top, Ms Wishbone ...'

c. says, 'And I can't understand why you never married.'

5. There is a new man at work, of whom the general consensus is 'A hunk, definitely a hunk.' In the course of business, you and he work together quite a bit, and you have to agree that he could probably make you forget about Zeke, the great love of your life who went off to India to bring solar energy to the people. So what if you and the hunk work together? you think. So what if the two of you will eventually be vying for the same promotion? So what if, though you do the same job and you have seniority, you have it straight from Thelma, the MD's secretary, that this man you would be happy to let play with your computer any time not only makes more than you do but is already in line for a company car? So what if he flirts with all the women in the office? They all flirt with him. You decide that a little direct action is called for. You are in his office one afternoon, and after your input on the monthly report has been duly completed, you say, 'You know, Matt, I was thinking that it might be nice if we had lunch together sometime.' He

a. says, 'Yeah, sure. That'd be great. I've been so busy trying to learn the ropes that I haven't had time to make any friends. But I'd certainly like you to be one of them.'

b. says, 'What about Friday? Somebody told me there's a great Italian restaurant not too far away. I'm sure nobody would mind if we were a little late getting back.'

c. says, 'I'm pretty booked up this week. Maybe towards the end of the month? Or maybe you'd fancy a little drink one night?'

If you normally selected a. as the response to which you would react most positively, then you are a person with her head screwed on right and her priorities straight. Of course, what Jane says is that a person who selected mainly a.s has no real gut-level determination, is wishy-washy and unadventurous and wouldn't know an opportunity if it came up, took her in its arms, bent her backwards over the piano, and declared its undying love. Jane says that irons aren't the only things that should cause you to strike while they're hot. 'Really, Serena,' says Jane, with that little huffy sound she sometimes makes, 'you're encouraging people to seek safety and to stay stuck in their ruts. I mean, really, humus sandwiches? Are you kidding or what?' I'm not kidding. For even if the chances for romance are slim with the a.s, the chances of a real friendship developing are good. And all of us know which category – boyfriends or real friends – has the longer shelf life. As Grandma Lucy, no small poet in her own way, once wrote on the occasion of a granddaughter's rather public separation from a husband (the granddaughter went after said husband and his new love with an electric carving knife at a Christmas party): oh, men they are flighty, and men they are fickle, stick to the friends who won't leave you in a pickle. If you're an a. person, your motives are pretty pure, and you bring out the honest and vulnerable in people effortlessly.

If you reacted most favourably to the b. answers, you are not only a hopeless romantic with limited judgment and no reliable early-warning system, you are asking to spend the next ten years of your life sitting up till all hours, crying along with

Dwight Yokum albums. 'Oh, steady on, Serena,' says Jane. 'What are you talking about? I thought the b.s had the most potential of the lot. They knew what they were after. They were ripe for a strong frontal assault.' That's what the Germans thought about the Eastern Front.

If c. was your letter you have definite romantic tendencies and are probably not distrustful by nature, but you do have at least a semi-working sense of self-preservation. You don't go for the obvious either way, but veer towards the shadows, waiting to see what happens next. There's a slight edge of Jane Fforbes-Smythe recklessness in you, but enough caution left to make you hedge your bets.

8

YOU MEET A HANDSOME PRINCE BUT NO SOONER DO YOU KISS HIM THAN HE TURNS INTO A FROG

People are always saying to me, 'I don't understand it, Serena. What goes wrong? I meet this really nice guy, we start talking about our jobs and our friends and films we've seen; we have a couple of dates and we get along just famously, you know, laughing at the same things and liking the same music and being able to share our meals because he likes the chips and I like the pickle. We become lovers, and that's even more wonderful, we have pillowfights and one-man panty raids, and we make such passionate love that the prints of cranes at sunset fall off the wall. And then, almost as soon as it's obvious that what we've got is serious, he starts changing.'

Sometimes he changes in little ways. Where at first he was always considerate – telephoning if he was going to be late, apologising if he forgot to do something he'd promised, asking you if you liked poached tripe before he started making supper – he suddenly starts to slip. He is three hours late for your party, and when he arrives claims that he fell asleep in the cinema. He gets held up at the office and doesn't think to call to tell you until hours after the soufflé has turned into a pancake and you've gone to bed. He decides to go away for the weekend without letting you know. He invites six people home for supper and expects you to do the cooking.

Sometimes he changes in bigger ways. The man who, when you first started going out, impressed you so much with his gentleness, turns into a creature who yells and screams and bangs his fist into the wall if the steak is too well-done or someone puts the orange juice container on the paper he's been working on.

The man who was at the beginning so understanding about your problems with your mother, your sister and your last boyfriend, starts saying things like, 'Oh, your mother's all right. You're the one who's childish', or 'I don't see why you should get upset because your sister didn't invite you over for Christmas dinner even if she did invite your brother. There's nothing that says she has to have you, too', or 'Are you sure you didn't provoke him into throwing the television through the front window?'

The man who once called you 'the sexiest, most arousingly gorgeous woman I have ever known' starts making jokes about your personal appearance. 'Let's face it, Ms Wishbone,' he smiles, giving you a little squeeze so you know he's sort of kidding, 'your thighs are to love handles what the Coca-Cola company is to fizzy drinks'; 'Oh come on honey,' he says, 'I wasn't being critical. I'm rather fond of your breasts.'

The man who had searched all his adult life for a woman of your intelligence and character starts criticizing you in public. 'For God's sake, don't ask Ms Wishbone what she thinks of Buñuel,' he says, at that dangerous curve in the dinner-party conversation when people have had too much to drink and have too little to say. 'Her favourite film of all time is *Bambi*.'

The man who wanted no more out of life than to make yours as happy as he could starts finding everything you ask him to do a burden. 'Help you paint the kitchen? I don't have time to paint the kitchen, Ms Wishbone. I've got to finish Act 3.' 'Drive you to the doctor's, Ms Wishbone? I can't take off from work to drive you to the doctor's. Take a cab if you think you'll have trouble getting in the bus with the cast.'

The first couple of times this happens, you think it must have been something to do with you. You think, well, maybe that remark I made about Richard Nixon was stupid. You think, well, maybe I do laugh like a horse. You think, so big deal, what if everyone knows I'm sensitive about the size of my nose? You do not think, hey, just one little minute here, it was my gypsy clothes and infectious laugh that first attracted him to me, why does he now find them an embarrassment and social liability? You think, maybe Roger's right and that blouse is cut a little low. You excuse yourself from the party and go into the bathroom to stare in the mirror at yourself from every angle, wondering if you are already beginning to look like your mother. Even though you distinctly remember saying, 'Now you will remember to pick me up at eight thirty, won't you, honey?' you will convince yourself that you are wrong, and that it is he – left all by himself at home with nothing to eat but some cold meat and cheese, worrying about where you might be so late at night in a blizzard – who has suffered, and not you, the person who wound up walking home.

Eventually, however, you begin to understand that it does not, in fact, have anything at all to do with you. You didn't start out smart and overnight become stupid. You didn't meet him when you were a cute and spunky person, and a few weeks later metamorphose into a dowdy slug. It didn't matter before you met him that you couldn't make beef goulash like his mother, and it doesn't matter now. If you think about it, you will realize that, with the exceptions of Ozzie Nelson and Robert Young, many men treat the woman they love as though they don't understand where they came from and they're too softhearted to ask them to leave. If you think about it, you will realize that what we have here is the classic example of the whore/madonna syndrome. A man is attracted to you because you enflame the tiny ember of wildness, sensuality and madness that still glows in his soul, buried underneath the years of social conditioning, the responsibilities and assumptions of his job, and his hopes that if he gives up smoking, drinks only at weekends, and invests wisely he will be able to retire comfortably at sixty and still have a few years in which to learn to play golf and read everything ever written by P.G. Wodehouse. But once he's got you, once you are no longer the dangerous temptress who makes love to him on the floor of the bathroom and comes behind him to kiss his back while he's on the telephone to his mother discussing the cat's bowel movements, but the woman he brings to office functions, friends' parties and his sister's Harvest Festival dinner, he doesn't want you to be fanning his embers, he wants you to be keeping the home fires burning, preferably dressed in something that would appeal to his mother. And once you are his, and under his tutelage, as it were, he seems to feel it is incumbent upon him to repair the lapses and errors in your education, to point out to you the 989 times a day when you are wrong and he is right.

In *My Fair Lady*, Henry Higgins asks the musical question: 'Why can't a woman be more like a man?' And a pretty good question it is, too. For men, as we all know, are logical and rational, practical and level-headed. They are physically stronger and better at bravery than their female counterparts. They are honest and unemotional, abhor gossip and backbiting, and would never dream of locking themselves in the bedroom all night just because someone close to them forgot their birthday.

The logic and rationality of men is, of course, self-evident. Who but a logical and rational creature would bring its planet to the brink of destruction? Who but a practical and level-headed being would raze the land, pollute the oceans and corrode the air? Who but the enemy of emotionalism and sentimentality would invent genocide?

Millions of women, children and small furry animals can attest to the physical strength and bravery of men.

Their intrinsic honesty ('My goodness, Janette, but you've certainly put on a lot of weight', 'Honey, honey, I swear I'll pull out'), their inspirational maturity (Krushchev pounding his shoe on the table at the UN, Nixon wiping the tears from his eyes as he announced that the media would no longer have him to kick around, Benny Lightfoot going into a six-day sulk when he found out that the wife he'd walked out on four years before was getting married again, notwithstanding), their abhorrence of gossip and back-biting are all well-documented.

But though one can sympathize that the strain for men of having to share an ever-shrinking world with fuzzy thinkers who are the playthings of their intuitions and feelings must be severe, there are times when a person can't help but think that Professor Higgins' question could be rephrased. You switch on the news and spend the next hour moving from one scene of war or famine to the next. You pick up the newspaper and are entertained with stories of young girls who went missing on their way home from the shops, toddlers found raped in ditches, the bombings of churches and hospitals and schools. You telephone your best friend, to cheer yourself up, and she tells you how the elderly woman next door was mugged by three young boys for the five pounds in her purse and a bottle of sherry. You phone your other best friend, who is usually good for a laugh, and she has a story about the man across the hall throwing the dog down the stairs because he was mad at his wife. It is at those times that you think about rejigging Henry's query. For instance, it might read: 'Why can't a man be more like a woman?' Or even: 'What possible evolutionary advantage could there be in having half of the species programmed to behave in such a way as to give baboons a bad name?'

Why Is It so Difficult for Men and Women to Understand One Another?

I don't know.

We go (for the most part) to the same schools, we watch the same television programmes, we see the same movies, we speak the same language, and yet it is often as though we inhabit parallel worlds. You speak to him, he speaks to you; you watch his lips move, he watches yours; you say, 'The potatoes are a little underdone,' and he knows exactly what you're talking about, the potatoes could have used another seven minutes in the pan. 'You're right,' he replies, 'the potatoes are a little underdone.' There, you think to yourself, we can communicate.

But then you go for something slightly trickier. You say, 'Geewhiz, what an awful week I've had at work, and then all the hullabaloo about my mother's bay tree being stolen, and the agony over whether or not the computer repairman was going to ask Annie out, and getting my speech ready for the award ceremony ... I'm pooped. I was really looking forward to seeing you this weekend, Mortimer, but I'm afraid we'll have to postpone. I just want to take it easy, potter around a little bit, maybe retype my speech one more time, and listen to Peruvian flute music. Why don't we make a date for Monday?' And Mortimer – who is aware of how hard you've been working all week, and who is aware of the hours you have spent, long into the night, assuring your mother that the police are very good on stolen bay trees, and who has agreed that it would be very nice if, after seven years, Annie was finally asked out on a date, and who has told you several times how proud he is that you won the Press Officer of the Year Award – listens to your words and thinks you said that you have more important things to do than go for a curry with him. Mortimer, who ummed and ahhed and oh-I-knowed while you spoke, who missed your brother's wedding because he had to take a client to a football game, believes that what you said was that you don't want to see him, probably because you've got a date with someone else. 'Well, sure,' he says. 'I understand what a busy woman you are, Ms Wishbone. Maybe I'll give Annie a ring and see if she wants to do something. I did tell you that she and I used to have a little thing, didn't I?' Or he doesn't say anything, but at eleven-forty-five, as you are curled up in front of the television with rags in your hair and cream on your face and a bowl of taco chips at your side, he turns up with a bottle of wine and a hard-on, obviously delighted to find you all on your own.

The first rule of dealing with men is to remember that anything that happens to them is important. If a man is ill he is really ill. Although the only time he visited you when you were in the hospital for a week was for thirty minutes the night his darts game was cancelled, if he has a temperature of 99 of you are expected to rush right over with a pile of magazines and a pot of soup. If you lose your job it is just one of those things, you can always go back to copy typing. But if he loses his job the world grinds to a halt. If a man has been hurt or insulted he has been permanently hurt and insulted and will carry the grievance with him to the grave, whereas you are childish because you hold it against his mother that she still calls you 'Audrey', the name of his first wife.

'Women,' my Uncle Conrad always says, 'like to think that they're the sensitive ones because they get all soppy when they see kittens or babies, and because they can still remember the dress they wore on the first day they ever went to school. That's poppycock,' Uncle Conrad continues. 'It's men who create the beautiful music and write the stirring poems and the moving plays and paint the lasting art. It's men who have real spirituality. Men are delicate creatures.'

And who would deny that? Although women do tend to get upset when their sons are sent off to be soldiers or someone makes an unkind remark about the lumpiness of the mashed potatoes, men are not without their soft underbelly. Their feelings can be hurt, too.

Take Annabelle's story. Annabelle and Pete had been living together for several years. In many ways, they had a good relationship, though it did, like so many, have its ups and downs. One day Annabelle and Pete were strolling down the street together, debating which film they were going to go and see, when they came upon a television showroom. There, on four different screens and in better than living colour, was Kelly McGillis. Pete stopped for a second, forgetting completely about all he had against films with subtitles, transfixed. Turning to Annabelle, Pete said, not without a little snippiness, 'Annabelle, why can't you look like Kelly McGillis?' Although this was a question that Annabelle had asked herself on more than one occasion, she was a little taken aback that it should suddenly be coming from a man who was so fond of sharing her shower. 'Well, Pete,' Annabelle replied, thinking as quickly as is possible for someone with an unclear mind, 'if I looked like Kelly McGillis I certainly wouldn't be living with you.' Pete reacted to this piece of information as though smote with a sharp and heavy instrument. 'How can you say a thing like that to me?' he protested. 'You know how sensitive I am,' the last words he spoke for the next week and a half, until his feelings had healed.

And men, of course, can never understand female jealousy. 'Women,' they say, rolling their piercing blue eyes, 'you spend a few minutes at a party talking to some very nice woman who needs advice on car insurance or you give a lift to one of the girls in the office who accidentally leaves her lipstick behind on the seat of the car, and all hell breaks loose.'

My friend Bob once turned up for our Friday night softball game with a black eye as big as the Isle of Wight. 'What happened to you?' I asked. 'One of your clients retaliate?' 'No,' said Bob, wincing and smiling at once, 'Wendy tried to kill me with that brass lamp her grandmother gave us for a wedding present.' 'Oh my God,' I said, genuinely shocked. 'What happened?' He winced again. 'She caught me in the act with another woman.' Bob then went on to explain his confusion and frustration with Wendy's actions. After all, they'd been together and blissfully happy for nearly ten years; she knew there would never be anyone else for him; this was just one of those physical things that don't count, that don't matter, but that it would be silly to pass up; he thought she'd understand; he thought, had he asked her, that she would have said, 'Sure thing, Bob, have a good time. Do you think she'll want to stay for supper?' Why are women so irrational and illogical? Why can't they understand that men need room and space?

No person in her right mind approves of jealousy. Jealousy is a negative and destructive emotion. Men say to women, 'Oooh, there is nothing that I hate more than a possessive and jealous woman. It's so childish. It's so demeaning. Love can only exist in an open relationship, founded on trust.' And women say back, 'You're right, I won't be jealous, it's old-fashioned and unattractive.'

But there are two types of jealousy. There is abstract jealousy, jealousy that exists more or less apropos of nothing – he's an hour late getting home from work so you immediately suspect him of having an affair. Abstract jealousy is not only a sign of madness, but it will eventually drive everyone around you mad as well. And then there is real jealousy. Real jealousy is based not on personal fantasies and the insecurity suffered as a child because both your parents were always too busy to build a bed for your Barbie Doll, but on the simple and well-documented fact that men are tricky and unreliable. If a woman gets a little red in the face and starts stomping around the kitchen, knocking glasses off the shelves, because her husband has left the party celebrating their fifteenth wedding anniversary to drive Mary Wapshott home, it is not because she begrudges Mary the ride just because her legs are six-feet long and she has hair the colour of salt-free butter, but because the wife knows that her husband would not have left the party to drive ten miles in a snow storm to take Sally Lipinski (who has normal-sized legs, salt-and-pepper hair and an unfortunate facial resemblance to Ernest Borgnine, and who at that very moment is calling for a cab) home. And because she knows why.

Trust us, men say, and then they bomb Poland, shoot down all the Indians, sell arms to Iran, or run off with Mary Wapshott.

Men's jealousy, on the other hand, is largely of the abstract variety. Few women will walk up to a stranger and sock her in the jaw because she's talking to the assailant's boyfriend. But a man will. Few women will time their husband's trips to the shop for bread or tonic water because she thinks that if he's twenty minutes later than he should be he must be up to no good. But a man will. Few women will pull the telephone out of the wall because a woman called asking (politely and with no untoward panting) to speak to John. But ...

Here's a thought question. Do men distrust women so much because they really believe:

a. that women are incapable of having a quick clinch in the broom cupboard without becoming emotionally involved, that unlike men they are not mature enough to separate their bodies from their emotions and so have to be constantly patrolled?

b. because they think women are so shallow, weak and sexually insecure that they will jump into bed with any man who speaks to them?

c. because they know themselves and their own behaviour so well that they can't believe that women don't act in exactly the same way?

How to Talk to Men

Men can be changed from princes to toads well before the kissing begins. You're sitting there across the table, gazing at him with incipient monarch-worship, thrilled with the tenor of his voice and the sweetness of his smile and the steadiness with which he wears his crown, and all of a sudden you say something ('No, it wasn't red, Helmut. It was green', or 'Really? Well I did my doctoral dissertation on Camus and I couldn't disagree with you more' or 'I know it's your job and all, but I'm really not that interested in the problems inherent in designing a hotel') and, poof!, there's a puff of smoke and you're staring into a pair of goggly eyes. Because of this, and because it may have been some time since you've been in the close proximity of any man who isn't a relative or in some service industry, you may need a little refresher course on how a person goes about talking to men.

'Isn't it just like talking to anybody else?' you ask in some surprise.

Not exactly.

It is one of those pieces of female folk-wisdom, passed down from generation to generation while hauling the water or stoking the fire or nursing the wounded soldiers, that men like to talk about themselves. When they are not talking about themselves they usually prefer to be left alone. A man certainly doesn't like to have to sit for hours and listen to some woman tell him about her job or the book she's been reading. Raised to common standards of politeness, most men will show a few minutes of interest in your new dress or your latest degree, and will listen attentively while you explain why you couldn't roast a chicken for dinner after all, but that is generally where their curiosity about you and your kind ends.

Women, of course, have long been taught that the way to get a man to like you is to show an interest in him that he will never show in you. Be a good listener. Ask him about himself. Get to know his interests. A hundred years ago, this was the sort of advice mothers were passing on to their daughters. Today it is the sort of advice that mothers are passing on to their daughters, friends to friends, and singles workshop leader to singles workshop.

'Oh, come on,' you say, 'I'm a tournament-level chess player, I built my own van, and I've travelled all over the world in a small sailing vessel with only my cat. I'm not going up to some guy in the office and ask him where he bought his socks.'

Jane says you are. Jane says that if you are sincere about not remaining a single person for the rest of your life you'd better start polishing up your conversational and listening skills right now.

'It's all very well and good knowing where to go to meet a man,' says Jane. 'But once you get there you've got to know what to say. Be practical. You may only have a matter of seconds to pique his interest.'

There are a million great opening lines – conversation starters that are to the ordinary 'And what do you do for a living, Joe?' what the neutron bomb is to the cap pistol.

'It must be difficult being so attractive to women.'

'You weren't by any chance in Bogotá in 1984, were you?'

'What's the best thing that ever happened to you?'

'If your eyes were grey instead of brown you'd be absolutely perfect.'

'Didn't you used to go out with Princess Caroline?'

'Have you ever had open-heart surgery?'

You are at the beach on a balmy summer's day. All around you are half-naked women with no hips, no stomachs and breasts that look like muffins. They are all cavorting here and there, laughing so their teeth show up against their tans. The sunlight sparkles against their sunglasses like stars. Also on the beach, along with the usual complement of obese middle-aged men wearing G-strings, skinny youths whose shorts always look like they're slipping down, and

men with young children draped over their shoulders, are one or two possible men who seem to be alone. They also seem to be paying a good bit of attention to the young women whose swimsuits don't seem to be covered by the *Oxford Dictionary*'s definitions of 'clothing'. How can you get the fellow in the straw hat and the pink sunglasses to pay some attention to you? You just walk right up to him and you say, 'Excuse me, but could I pick your brains for a minute? I was wondering what sort of retirement plan you have.' He peers at you over the rim of his glasses. 'Are you an insurance salesman?' he asks, sounding as puzzled as he looks. 'Oh no,' you say, 'no I'm not. It's just that I always thought I'd like to retire by the sea. Would you?'

Depending where you are at the time, it is usually easy enough to get a man to talk about himself. If you are standing by a car you can ask him what sort of antifreeze he uses. If you are in a bakery you can ask him if he prefers rye bread with seeds or without ('Oh,' you say, with your adorable grin, 'I thought you looked like a seed man. How do you feel about cream cakes?') If you are on a bridge you can ask him why it doesn't snap in the middle. The important thing – as Jane, my mother, my grandmother, and my great-grandmother would point out – is to ask him something that will make him feel superior. It is unnecessary to ask him only about things you feel confident he knows something about. Most men will give you an opinion whether they know anything about the subject or not.

As Dr Jekyll found upon creating Mr Hyde, however, starting a man talking is often easier than getting him to stop. Once he's loping along, telling you about his years on the road as a timer-switch salesman, he will pick up momentum. And once he's left the relatively finite shores of the utilitarian world and entered the infinite universe of himself, the brake mechanism has been known to fail completely. My friend Jenny tells of dating a man who took her on a floating restaurant. At eight o'clock the boat started up the river, and at one or two ('Or four or five,' said Jenny. 'It was the first time I really understood that phrase "and time stood still" ') it came back to its mooring. It was meant to be romantic. Out on the river, the stars twinkling overhead and a band playing soft music, a fully stocked bar, excellent wine list and rich sauces on everything. 'It was like a cruise through hell,' said Jenny. 'How many times can you excuse yourself to go to the ladies'? And even if he believed my story about inheriting my mother's weak bladder, I figured once an hour was about the limit. I mean, Serena, imagine it. I couldn't get a headache and go home. I couldn't sneak out the back way and leave him a note with the waiter.' It was a first date, arranged (significantly enough) by Jane Fforbes-Smythe, who had met the gentleman in question while out purchasing fishing tackle. He was too tall for Jane, but they struck up a friendship anyway, and in the end Jane introduced him to Jenny. 'Every time he paused I asked him something else about himself,' said Jenny. 'And what's your favourite type of casserole, Gus? And how big is the average trout you catch? Would you ever shoot anyone deliberately? And then I realized that I didn't have to ask him anything for the next five hours. He was telling me about the wallpaper he had in his room when he was ten, and I thought, uh oh, pretty soon he's going to start telling me about his first girlfriend, and barely had the thought blipped through my brain than he started telling me about going fishing with Sheila and always having to bait her hook for her. By the time we reached the coffee and brandy I was ready to eat the tablecloth.'

PART II

How to Meet Men

9

TRADITIONAL WAYS OF MEETING MEN

Okay, so you've had enough of solitaire, have read all the great works of literature, and if you take one more self-improvement class you will be so incredibly terrific that there won't be a man left on earth worthy of eating your leftovers.

Okay, so you know men are not as easy to live with as tropical plants or your average African Grey parrot, but you've decided to put up with the inconvenience and bother for the sake of having an ear to nibble on nights when you're feeling frisky. And, just maybe, to stop yourself from getting depressed on those other nights, when you suddenly realize that you're the only uncoupled person on the planet.

Okay, you know you've had some disastrous relationships in the past (Howard, the neat freak, who couldn't sleep if the sheets weren't ironed; Stewie, the hopeless romantic, who would remember the day you met with flowers and Bloody Marys, but would forget to pay the rent; Damion, the loner, who would go out for a newspaper and come back six weeks later wanting to know where you'd put that book he was reading; Jack, the great lover, who turned out to be loving everyone else as well ...), but you are willing to put all that behind you. You are not going to let the past colour your attitude towards men in the future. This time is going to be different.

But before it can be different, of course, you've got to meet someone.

'And how am I supposed to do that with the drought upon us?' you would like to know.

All the experts, from my mother to Jane, are agreed that the only thing standing between you and meeting the man of your dreams is yourself.

My mother, a long-time advocate of the traditional approach to meeting men, would say that you're not taking enough initiative. You are being stubborn, just like you were when you were little and refused to wear those patent leather shoes to Mary Rooney's birthday party because you were sure all the other girls would be wearing (as opposed to dating) Cuban heels. There is nothing wrong with getting a little outside help, says my mother. That's what friends and families are for. If your friend Sally has a single brother who walks on his back legs and has never been in jail, why shouldn't you meet him? If Mrs Simpson's handsome nephew, the widowed building baron, is going to be at Mrs Simpson's birthday party, what's the harm in you making an appearance as well? If your sister knows a man at work who is just your type and is even a vegetarian, just like you, what possible objection could you have to meeting him for a drink or a film? Do you think your sister would match you up with the monster that ate Chicago? Decide what sort of man you're looking for (professional, older, younger, sporty, good with his hands, creative), and then decide where you are most likely to find him (always taking into consideration, of course, the fact that he might just turn up at Lucinda's wedding because his car broke down outside or he once shared a flat with the groom).

My mother has successfully placed two daughters,

one niece, the only child of her best friend and the doctor's receptionist using her methods. Jane has known (or heard of) approximately five hundred people who have found their ideal mates through modern means – and though she is not yet herself one of the lucky ones, she has, she maintains, come close on more than one occasion. 'At least I have dates,' says Jane.

The traditional ways of meeting men come from a time when communities were close and families extended. They rely on the personal touch, on people who know you matching you up with someone they are sure you will like. They rely on the idea that in a small world the people who meet one another will have certain things in common. Jane says that though she has always admired my mother's success rate with the traditional method (and does not hold it against her that the one man she found for Jane turned out to be allergic to her), it is only good as far as it goes – and in these desperate times it doesn't go quite far enough.

The Blind Date

Quite frankly, though I am astounded to hear myself say that I know of at least one blind date that ended in an extremely happy marriage, my personal attitude to them is that anybody who was sane would rather be in Philadelphia. I myself (despite my mother's and my Aunt Beryl's most strenuous efforts) have only even been on one blind date in my life, a long time ago but I can still remember every detail of it much as a person will remember till the day she dies exactly what everybody was wearing, doing, and saying on the Amsterdam ferry the afternoon that Jack Shepard told her that though he didn't want to spoil her holiday by cancelling beforehand, he did think that she should

know that it was over between them, long after the specifics of much better experiences have totally vanished from her mind.

There are two reasons why blind dates are more risky than hang gliding. The first is that, just as a recipe depends on the cook, the successful blind date depends on the arranger.

'Well, I don't see why that should be a problem,' you say. 'Obviously, if someone is setting up a date for you that person must know you well enough to understand your tastes and interests and what sort of men you like.'

You'd think so, wouldn't you? And it is true that, like most murders, most blind dates are committed by people who know the victims fairly well. And yet my own mother has tried her damnedest to get me to go out with a man who played a rabbit in a television commercial ('He once worked with Olivier. His mother says he's a brilliant actor'), her assistant bank manager ('He told me he reads *Lucky Jim* every year, for pleasure. Now that's really something, isn't it?'), and the man who came to investigate when she saw the flying saucer land in the back garden ('He's very sensible, Serena, not at all what you think').

Anyone who has decided to have a dinner so that her three best friends can meet at last has already discovered that: 1. your three best friends will loathe one another; and 2. each of your three best friends will have a totally different view of you, so different that they might each be friends with a different person. That is why friends trying to find the perfect man for you will, nine times out of ten, come up with the last man on earth you would ever want to get stuck in a lift with.

Oh, they say, Ms Wishbone has such a great sense of humour, let's tell Chuck to give her a ring. Chuck, of course, is a clown who tells jokes that amuse at the rate of about five knots a minute. He talks in funny voices to the waiter. He has a laugh that makes everyone around you smile as though they've just swallowed a fly.

Oh, they say, Ms Wishbone is interested in the Orient, she and Reggie would probably get on like a forty-four room mansion going up in smoke. Reggie, it turns out, is nicknamed Bunny and spent several years in that bastion of Chinese culture, Hong Kong, merchant banking. He speaks several words of Cantonese, but none of them any lady would want to know.

Oh, they say, hasn't Ms Wishbone travelled all over the world with just a backpack and an indomitable spirit, don't you think she and Alex would make a good team? Alex (what else?) is a travel agent who specializes in the Costa Brava.

The only thing worse than your friends trying to fix you up with the man of your dreams is your relatives trying to gun him down. At least your friends do have some idea of what you're really like as a person. Your friends know that though when you were eight years old the very appearance of a spoonful of spinach on the edge of your plate was enough to make you gag, you now quite enjoy it in soufflés and crêpes and mixed with dill rice. Your friends don't think that because you asked for a chemistry set for your thirteenth birthday that you'd necessarily be interested in dating a chemical engineer. Your friends know about your secret love of country music. Your friends know that you have had sex. Your friends know that it only takes four tequila sunrises and a Flaco Jiménez song to have you dancing on the table and singing the chorus in Spanish. Where a friend will only think that she or he knows what's best for you better than you yourself, families know that they know. 'I know Ms Wishbone's always been a little wild,' says Mrs Wishbone. 'A little bohemian, if you know what I mean. There was that sociology professor and the guitarist with the beard, remember? And of course she will insist on gallivanting all over and always settling in big cities like Rome and London and New York. But I'm sure that once she got to know Jeffrey and saw how successful his photocopying centre is and what a nice house he has in Milton Keynes, then she'd change her mind'.

The second reason why blind dates are usually less pleasant than a root canal is the datee himself. 'Where do they find them?' my friend Jenny, who's been on more blind dates than I've been on adult education courses, wants to know. 'You think there's a vault somewhere, safe from the everyday world and normal people, where they keep them until they need them? Sort of like frozen sperm?'

'No, no,' said Liza, who didn't speak to her brother

for three years after he set her up with a Hell's Angel as a joke. 'With the exception of Ape Man, most of these guys are perfectly normal, average, and reasonable in daylight. You'd pass them on the street and not think, oh my God, I bet every time he eats a bowl of soup he gets his tie wet. They talk about the weather and where they get their shoes repaired and what they think is going to happen in the Middle East, and they give you a hand putting your groceries in the car, so your friends have no idea what they're really like. Just because you see a guy at work every day for two years doesn't mean that you know what he keeps in his fridge or under his bed. It's only when the moon comes out and they're put in the path of a possible conquest that the hair starts to grow between their toes and they can't stop talking about the years they spent in the marines.'

'But some blind dates aren't so bad, right?' you ask.

Right. At least one in every four or five thousand.

A Typical Blind Date

A telephone rings.

SHE: Hello?

HE: Hello. May I please speak to Darla Henning?

SHE: This is Darla Henning speaking. Who is this?

HE: Hello? Darla? Darla, you don't know me? My name's Hal Bog? I'm a friend of your friends Jane and John?

SHE: (slightly mesmerized by the rhythm of his queries) You are?

HE: Yes, I am. Didn't Jane tell you I was going to call?

SHE: (straining to recapture the vague and fleeting memory of Jane finishing off the third pitcher of martinis with a, 'Oh, yeah, did I tell you about the new guy John works with?') Oh yes, yes, Jane did say something about it.

HE: Well, here I am, calling.

After a preliminary conversation in which both parties give a little relevant information about themselves (he's an atomic physicist, she's a Professor of Medieval Studies known for her green bread festivals; he loves Japanese food, she loves Tex-Mex; he's a big Woody Allen fan – 'You mean you're tall?' she quips, and he says, 'Huh?' – she likes Frank Capra; he didn't see that special on Lapland, she did), they agree to go out on a date.

SHE: How will I recognize you?
HE: (looking in the mirror near his telephone, suddenly realizing that it is difficult to describe something with which you are on intimate terms) Recognize me?
SHE: Yes, recognize you. What do you look like?
HE: Well, I'm sort of fair, and I have grey eyes, and I don't have a moustache or a beard or anything like that.
SHE: (taking notes) Uh huh.
HE: I'm not fat, but I'm not really skinny either.
SHE: Right. Sort of fair, grey eyes, no facial hair, average weight. Anything else? Body building? Earring? Scars? Tattoos?
HE: Yes, there's one more thing.
SHE: (holding her breath – she has always rather fancied the idea of a man with a black eye patch, or even a hook instead of a left hand) Uh huh.
HE: I look as though I should be taller.

Darla recognizes Hal the second she walks into the bar. Not only does he look, indeed, as though he should be taller, but he is the only man there who is staring at the door as though he is Aladdin, waiting for something to happen with the lamp. She tries to gauge from the expression in his eyes whether he is elated at the sight of her, relieved, or struck dumb with disappointment. She wonders if she should have worn her jeans, or if she should have worn something dressier. Hal is wearing a suit. She wonders if the cossack shirt and gaucho pants are too ethnic. Hal looks like a car salesman. She tries to appear calm and natural and at the same time determine whether she is relieved at the sight of him (she is definitely not elated), or struck dumb with disappointment (if he sold cars, the cars he sold would be used).

HE: Darla?

SHE: (Fighting her way across the crowded room and managing to step on someone's toes and have a quarter pint of beer spilt on her in the process) Hal! Hello at last.

HE: Can I get you a drink? (he finishes off his second whisky and soda, grateful to see that his hand has stopped shaking – and wondering what the hell it is she's wearing)

SHE: That would be wonderful. Thank you. That would be great.

HE: (waving at the barman, who can't see him because he's so short) What's your poison?

SHE: What are you having? (being charitable, she has decided to assume that he doesn't normally talk like this, as she doesn't normally talk like this. She feels as though she's in the pilot of a new television sit com. One whose option isn't going to be taken up)

HE: Whisky and soda. With ice.

SHE: (squinching up her nose thoughtfully) I'll have a white wine.

HE: (to the bartender, who is only sort of looking in his direction) Ahem. Can we have one whisky and soda with ice and a white wine, please? Dry, Darla?

SHE: (nobly resisting the temptation to make the obvious joke) Yes, please, Hal.

HE: Excuse me. Excuse me, but do you think we could have a whisky and soda with ice and a dry white wine? (mumbling) If that's not too much trouble?

SHE: It certainly is crowded in here.

HE: Excuse me ... I say ... Can you believe this place, Darla? I've never seen it this crowded before.

SHE: (ducking as a tray of drinks is passed over her head) No, Hal, I can't believe it. Boy is it crowded.

HE: (rising on his toes as unobtrusively as possible; shouting) Excuse me, but do you think someone could wait on us here? We've been here some time.

They finally get their drinks. There are no vacant stools or tables, of course, so they huddle together in a corner near the door. Neither of them had realized how cold it is tonight. Even though the jukebox is at the other side of the room, the bar is so full that it is difficult to hear what you yourself are saying, let alone anyone else.

HE: So, Darla, how's your drink?

SHE: Pardon me?

HE: I said, how's your drink?

SHE: Oh, fine, Hal, just fine. (it tastes like newt piss, something she knows because she has five brothers)

HE: So, Darla, you're into the Middle Ages, huh? That must be very interesting.

SHE: Yes, Hal, yes it is. I'm especially interested in the relationship between science and religion. I think it has a lot to teach us that is relevant today.

HE: You enjoy teaching, do you?

SHE: Teaching?

HE: Well, yes, I have done some myself, actually. But I'm happier in the lab.

SHE: Your work must be incredibly fascinating, Hal.

HE: (this he hears) Oh it is, Darla. It is. Do you know much about quantum mechanics?

SHE: (unable to stop herself) No, Hal, no I don't.

HE: Oh well I'll try to explain it in layman's – or laywoman's – terms for you. Picture this if you can ...

By the time Hal has finished explaining all about Schrödinger's cat, it is too late to go to the cinema and almost too late to go to the restaurant. By the time they do get to the restaurant, neither of them can think of much to say. Tipsy as he is, Hal did notice that Darla's attention seemed to wander when he was telling her the amazing story of Heisenberg's hayfever, and Darla is wondering why she isn't at home, watching *Fawlty Towers* on the video and setting her hair.

HE: (as they take their seats beneath a fig tree of almost biblical proportions) This is the best Italian restaurant in town, Darla. You know who I've seen eating here? Would you believe Dustin Hoffman? John Cleese? Dr Edward Cruickshank?

SHE: Edward who?

HE: Edward Cruickshank, the elementary-particle physicist. Did I tell you that I once worked with him at Princeton?

SHE: No. No, surprisingly enough, you didn't tell me that.

Despite the unaccustomed alcoholic distortion, he can still tell that this evening is stretching before them like a holiday in a black hole. He is not used to conversing with non-colleagues, especially female non-colleagues, especially female non-colleagues who are dressed like extras in *Ivan the Terrible*. He is used to

women taking an interest in him – asking him
questions, looking awed at his answers, wanting to
know his opinion on God. She is afraid to look at her
watch in case it makes her burst into tears. The
ordering itself takes twenty minutes, because Hal, with
the thoroughness and curiosity of a scientist, has to
check with the waiter that everything he is ordering is
fresh ('And the mozzarella, is it fresh?' 'Yes, sir, of
course.' 'And the basil, it is fresh, isn't it?' 'Of course,
signor. The chef grows it himself.' 'And what about the
veal, then?' 'Slaughtered out back just this morning.')

HE: (breaking a breadstick in half and sniffing it) So,
      Darla, have you ever been to Italy?
SHE: Yes, Hal, as a matter of fact, yes I have.
HE: Florence?
SHE: Yes, I've been to Florence.
HE: I like Florence.
SHE: I do too.
HE: Venice?
SHE: Oh, yes. I love Venice. It's my favourite city. I
      lived there for over a year.
HE: A year? Really? I don't know how you could have
      stood it. I know everyone always goes gaga about
      Venice, but I have to say that I for one found it
      very claustrophobic.
SHE: Did you?
HE: Yes. It is pretty, mind you, but so cramped. I can't
      believe you didn't find it claustrophobic.
SHE: Well, I was young and unsophisticated then. I'm
      sure I would have found it claustrophobic if I'd
      been with you.
HE: (relaxing in his first compliment of the evening)
      Waiter! Another bottle of wine, please.

   The meal goes slowly. Hal sends back the insalata
tricolore because the tomatoes are over-ripe. Hal sends
back the veal picata because it's overcooked. Hal sends

back the coffee. Darla tries to send the waiter telepathic messages of sympathy, but from the way he sneers when he says, 'And the sugar, signor, does that seem fresh enough to you?' she assumes that he isn't receiving them. Over the dessert, Hal starts to tell her about his tempestuous and doomed affair with Lorna, the test-tube salesperson and great love of his life.

HE: (having brought his chair around so that they can look at the pictures he carries in his wallet together) And this is me and Lorna at the beach. You can see how happy we were that day.

SHE: She's very pretty.

HE: She's beautiful.

SHE: And where was this one taken?

HE: That's the university car park.

SHE: Oh, and here's the university car park with no one in it.

HE: That was after she drove away. It was the last time I ever saw her.

SHE: (passes him her napkin, which, having spent most of the evening on the floor, is still clean)

HE: Do you think I should have gone after her and made her listen to reason? The last woman I went out with thought I should have. But she seemed so adamant – Lorna, that is, not the woman who thought I should have gone after her – that I didn't know what to do. I'd never seen her violent before.

SHE: (passes him a napkin from the table behind them)
   Darla takes Hal home in a taxi. She sees him to his door.

HE: Well, good night, Darla. Thank you for a very nice evening. You've been very helpful. You're a good friend.

SHE: Oh, that's all right. I've had a very … uh … interesting time.

HE: I'll call you.

SHE: Oh, didn't I tell you? I'm just off to Jerusalem to
     do some research on the Crusades. I'll ring you
     when I get back. Do give Jane and John my love.

There is one hard and fast rule when it comes to blind
dates. And this is it: unless you are absolutely positive
beyond even the tiniest shadow of a doubt that the
Mrs Springsteen your Aunt Betty met when she took
that package tour to Atlantic City has just the one son,
his name is Bruce and he plays the guitar, don't go.

Your Mother, Your Relatives, Your Mother's Friend Who Had the Hip Operation

The dates and prospective bridegrooms that are foisted
on you by caring relations and the friends of caring
relations are so closely linked in your mind with the
blind date that you probably can't imagine why your
mother maintains that she would never, not in a
million years, be involved in arranging one.

'What?' your mother says, turning from the stove
with a look of horror in the maternal eye. 'You're going
on a blind date? You're going out with a man you don't
know? Who could be anybody? Who could be a sex
maniac? Who could be one of those men who strangles
you with your own tights and then writes HA HA on
the bathroom mirror with your lipstick? What's got
into you? Is this the way we brought you up? Is this
what the dancing lessons, and the violin lessons, and
the corrective brace were all for?'

'Mother,' you say, 'I know I've never met him
before, but it's not like he's a complete stranger. He is
Angela Murgotroyd's cousin, after all. I've known
Angela since we were five. I don't think she'd

encourage me to go out with her favourite relative if she thought he likes dressing up as a school girl and being hit on the fanny with an exercise book.'

Your mother sniffs. 'In my day,' lies your mother, 'this sort of thing was unheard of. A woman didn't go with just anyone. Men are like shellfish, you can't be too careful.'

By the time the day arrives for your date with Angela's cousin, you have had heavy phonecalls from every female relation you have, as well as from your mother's best friend, Maureen (whose own daughter ran off with a mini-cab driver who got her pregnant and then went back to his wife). Your sister remembers the time Angela convinced you to help her steal *The Joy of Sex* from the library, and that you were the one who got caught because you were the one out of whose jumper it dropped right in front of the librarian's desk. 'Is this the sort of person you trust?' your sister inquires. Your grandmother recalls that there was a very famous murder case involving a Murgotroyd in the early nineteenth century. 'How can you be sure they're not related?' she wants to know. Your aunt has not forgotten that Angela once lived in Goa with an Argentinian hippy who designed clothes that lit up and who had a small sideline in controlled substances.

And yet these are the same people who are constantly offering you men of all ages, sizes, colours and conditions. (Male relatives, thank God, rarely participate in this activity – unless, that is, you come from a culture where the father traditionally arranges your marriage for you when you are six, in which case you aren't reading this book. Normally, fathers don't like to get embroiled in the *Sturm und Drang* of their daughters' lives any more than they like to be told the details of diaphragm insertion or to be asked to stop by on the way home and pick up a box of tampons. Brothers occasionally volunteer a friend or classmate or flying buddy who has seen a family picture and thought you 'didn't look bad', but on the whole when they are young they can't imagine why anyone would want to date their sister and when they are older they still can't. But your mother only has to sit next to a woman on the bus with a son your age and before she's reached her destination she's given you away.

From one point of view, this strong interest that mothers, sisters, grandmothers, aunts and even close cousins show in swapping children with anybody they meet is an annoyance.

For one thing, it means that you are never safe at any family gathering. There you are, draped with tinsel and curling ribbon and wrapping paper with snowflakes and Santas on it, well-tucked into your fourth glass of Christmas champagne, and feeling pretty pleased with yourself because you have opened all your presents without flinching, when all of a sudden you hear your sister say in a voice as bright as an aluminium tree, 'Oh, Mum, did I tell you who I bumped into the other day?'

Immediately, your early-warning system is activated and you wonder if you should switch to whisky right now. You look around to see if your father is near the drinks table and realize that he has left the room.

'Derek,' says your sister, practically singing. 'Derek Hamilton.'

'Derek Hamilton?' asks your mother in a puzzled tone, as though she is not a woman with the memory of an industrial computer.

'Yes, Derek Hamilton,' says your sister, glancing over very quickly to make sure that you haven't followed your father. 'You remember him. Tall, dark, absolutely gorgeous looking. Got a First at Oxford. Captain of the cricket team. Won a scholarship to study medicine at Harvard. Was on the cover of *Newsweek* for a project he started in some slum or something like that. You remember.'

All this time, your mother's and your sister's eyes

have not made contact.

'You don't mean the Derek Hamilton who was always so sweet on Ms Wishbone, do you?' asks your mother.

You look wildly towards the door, but, alas, it is too late. Your Aunt Beryl is stationed stoutly before it, a tray of cheese straws and stuffed dates held before her like a shield. 'Oh wasn't he just?' pipes in Aunt Beryl, smiling at you encouragingly.

'Well, what do you know about that,' says your mother. 'Imagine. After all these years. How is Derek now?'

'Oh wonderful, wonderful,' enthuses your sister. And then her voice drops just a little and becomes slightly softer, as though she is about to impart some tragic news and ruin everyone's Christmas.

You knock back your drink and reach for the bottle. There's no time to get up and retrieve the whisky.

'But very lonely, of course,' your sister is saying. 'He's only just come back to this country, and his family is scattered all over the globe, and he's been so immersed in his career, you know, that he hasn't had a chance to marry and start a family of his own.'

Her eyes, as are the eyes of your aunt, your grandmother and your mother, are on you as you pull a recalcitrant cork out with your teeth.

'Oh, the poor man,' says your mother. 'And he was always so nice. Kind and considerate, wouldn't you say so, Beryl?'

'Oh, yes,' says Beryl, 'the soul of consideration. Don't you think so, Mother?'

'He was all right,' says your grandmother. 'I never cared for his uncle, though. The one they had to send to Canada.'

There are a few seconds of silence, while your closest female relatives all smile at you, their gazes calculating and expectant. The cork pops.

'He asked after you,' says your sister. And even

though you are deliberately not looking at her, you know, somehow, that she isn't speaking to your mother.

'Oh,' says your mother.

'Um,' says Aunt Beryl.

'That's nice,' says Grandma.

'He wanted to know if you ever married,' says your sister.

Your memory of Derek Hamilton is slightly different to that of the rest of the family. Although he did get a First at Oxford, and he was, as you recall, captain of the cricket team, and he did win a scholarship to Harvard, and though you have no doubt that he was probably on the cover of *Newsweek*, so were Henry Kissinger and Idi Amin. Derek Hamilton was handsome in a way that always made you think of Nazi officers. You can't imagine him doing anything in a slum unless it was to be a landlord. You take a quick slug of champagne, and then you say as much. You say, 'Derek Hamilton was one of the most stuck-up, conceited, pontificating balloon-brains it has ever been my misfortune to meet, and if anyone wants to know why I never married they need look no further than the two dates I had with him.'

Your sister holds out her glass for a refill. 'Well,' she says, in the same voice she once used to tell you that because you had slept two nights in a row in your underwear your parents were going to send you to an orphanage, 'I do hope you're not too drunk to watch that negative attitude of yours, because as it happens I invited him to join us for dinner and that's probably him at the door right now.'

From another point of view, however, this ability to conjure men out of short train journeys, shopping jaunts, emergency visits to the launderette, and implanted wisdom teeth is nothing short of miraculous. How is it that you – bright, vivacious, attractive, and possessor of a smouldering sensuality that is kept in control only with the fiercest willpower – can spend six hours at a crowded, drunken, sexually active party, listening intently with a look of keen interest on your face to very long and very intricate descriptions of runaway wives, the correct way to smoke your own eels, trips to Sweden to watch for UFOs, and the telephone system in Thailand, and being a good sport about dancing to disco and hip hop and not demanding rock-and-roll, and yet the only eligible man you meet is visiting from Paraguay and doesn't speak English. But your mother – who, though certainly a charmer in her way and a woman of many fine qualities, is a little on the matronly, small and roundish side and has once or twice been mistaken for a cuddly toy – your mother has only to bump shopping trolleys by the cheese counter and she's got the address, phone number and polaroid picture of a thirtyish, single television producer who wants nothing more (according to his mother) than to find the woman of his dreams and settle down somewhere with enough land to be able to have a pony for the kids.

Besides acting as marriage brokers, your mother, sisters, grandmothers, cousins and aunts and their well-wishers provide a natural and indefatigable support group. Unlike your best friend, your mother will not steam round at ten o'clock on a night of crisis with a bottle of wine, a bowl of homemade salsa, a crate of nacho chips and the video of *Tootsie* to cheer you up, but (unlike your best friend, who sometimes has to pay some attention to the problems in her own life) your mother will never cease her efforts on your behalf (you, single and way past the age when if you were olive oil you'd be called virgin, are her problems).

'Go to the wedding,' she says. 'It doesn't matter if you wore that cream dress and the little blue hat with the quail feathers to the last three weddings, you never meet the same men twice, who's going to remember?'

'Go to the company outing,' she advises. 'You never know who will turn up. You've got nice legs. It'll give you a chance to show them off.'

She'll make sure no other daughter of hers has a dinner party that features even one single male of good character that doesn't include you.

She'll keep an eye on your diet. ('Another piece of chocolate cake, Ms Wishbone? Do you think Jamie Lee Curtis has that body because she eats two helpings of moussaka for dinner and then wolfs down half a fudge cake for dessert?')

She'll make sure that there is no way of your missing crucial calls because of the ineptitude of the telephone company ('I was got out of bed this morning by a repairman who said somebody had reported a fault on my line. That wasn't you, by any chance, was it, Mother?').

Your mother, at far less cost than a year's subscription to all the major women's magazines, will advise you of any areas in your life where you may be weak ('I don't know how you ever expect to find a man with that temper', 'Do you think any man is going to want to live with a woman who keeps seventeen rubber ducks in the bath?').

All of this is, as I have already pointed out, a hangover from earlier times, when extended families lived together in one hut and major life decisions were not left to chance but made by the elders. One night, as you were getting ready to crawl under your smelly old bearskin, your mother would come up to you with a young man in tow, and say something like, 'Ms Wishbone, this is Tuhuana, maybe you've seen him around. He's young and brave, has few scars and most of his teeth. He's brought half an elk and four spears with him as presents for our group, and from now on you're his woman. Be fertile.'

It is not such a bad thing, really, to think that here, deep in the private parts of the rumbunctious twentieth century, some remnants of these old traditions linger. Nor, according to no less an authority than Jane, is this method of meeting men to be entirely scoffed at. Just as every once in a while there is a blue moon or a double rainbow, just as in the middle of the most gruesome war there will be a moment of peace, the men on both sides putting down their arms and meeting together in brotherhood to sing 'Silent Night' and share out the chocolate bars, just as flowers bloom in the desert and a person with a big nose may be given the sexiness of Marlene Dietrich, just so, not all of the men your mother comes upon are going to be candidates for the Lame-o Hall of Fame.

'Face it,' says Jane, 'even Dustin Hoffman has a mother.'

Your Friends

Here's what happens. You're talking to your best friend on the telephone one night, and after you've exchanged the updates on what's been happening in each of your lives (she's just been put on the board of directors, you've just been asked to write a screenplay for Robert Redford, her toilet is flushing hot water, your blender exploded under suspicious circumstances) and your friends' lives (Angie is talking about leaving Ben again, Sue is on a diet, Alicia wonders if it is too late to go back to school, Paula was asked out on a date by Bono, but it was her yoga night so she didn't go), and after you've discussed the films you've seen recently, the plays that you've been to and the good books you've read, she says, 'So it's four tablespoons of coriander in the salsa, right?' You say, 'Right. Heaped.' And she says, 'Great. Oh, I almost forgot. There's someone I want you to meet.'

The first few times this little scenario takes place,

you feel a surge of girlish excitement. Certainly you feel interested. Hopeful even. After all, who knows you better than your best friend? Here is a person who shares your passions for Katherine Hepburn films, silver bracelets, bean and potato burritos, Crazy Horse, Beethoven, Emmy Lou Harris, slinky dresses, seamed black stockings and men who wear undershirts. It is impossible that she would ever introduce you to a dork. Isn't it?

Unfortunately, as we have already talked about apropos the blind date, it is not impossible at all. And if you think about all the times you have said to one friend about the boyfriend/husband/paramour of another, 'I mean, he's a nice guy and all that, but I don't see what she sees in him. If I go over there one more time and he tells me the joke about the Basque fisherman or plays that Woody Guthrie album, I swear I'll hit him,' you will realize that you have said it in connection with every friend you've ever had, barring, maybe, one. Or you have said something similar, like, 'Well, no, he's not much to look at and he does have that unfortunate habit with his teeth, but you can see that Marilyn needed somebody really secure and stable after Derek. I mean, I can't imagine playing porpoises with him, but he is quiet and he did cook the supper.' The times you have said, 'God knows what she sees in that jerk.' The times you have said, 'It'll never last.' And your friends, of course, have often said the same sorts of thing about you. 'What's Ms Wishbone doing with that deadbeat?'

Despite all this, one's friends go on trying. Even though they themselves may be living with men who are less than anyone's ideal and may secretly envy you your freedom and independence. 'Lucky Ms Wishbone,' they say to themselves, 'when she gets home from work or a pleasant evening with friends, she can kick off her shoes and collapse on the sofa with a gin and tonic and a bag of crisps. The cat will snuggle next to her. She can watch anything she wants to on television. She won't have to feign interest for three hours in the fluctuations of the international stock market before she's allowed to go to bed. When she gets to bed, she won't have to play hide and seek with Heman the penis for fifteen minutes before she can get to sleep.' No matter how unsatisfactory their own home lives, however, they are always on the lookout for your possible partner. Is it because they're tired of being the ones doing all the complaining and would like to give you a turn?

The only thing to remember when your best friend says, 'Come over to supper on Thursday, I've got someone I'm just dying for you to meet,' is not to get your hopes up. Remember the time she threw a summer solstice party so you could meet this great guy who turned out to be a manic depressive who took you back to his place to show you all the holes he'd punched in the walls? Remember how many broken hearts you've had to see her through? Go thinking not, I'm about to meet a man who looks like Robert de Niro and can play 'Girls from Texas' on the guitar, but, I'm about to get a free meal and with any luck she'll make that chocolate pie I like so much. Keep in mind that God does work in some pretty mysterious ways, and so, as Chuck Berry once noted, you never can tell. You might get really lucky.

I cite the story of my friend Lana as an example. Lana's friend, Joan, invited her to dinner one evening. Joan not only said, 'Wait'll you meet this guy. I swear to heaven you were made for each other,' but 'Wear those heels with the ankle straps and the taffeta mini skirt with the sequinned top.' So Lana did. Although she was only going to Joan and Waldorf's for spaghetti with pesto sauce, she dressed as though she were going to the Emmy Awards with Prince. She had her legs waxed. She spent the year's wages of a Bolivian peasant on a haircut and perm. She went to the dentist

and had her teeth cleaned. When the Jehovah's Witnesses came to the door she practiced listening intently and with interest, instead of suddenly shouting out that there was something burning on the stove and slamming the door in their faces.

Lana was really excited. This was going to be it. After all, Joan herself is not only married to a truly wonderful man, but she had never before been known to dabble in matchmaking. Which, Lana realized well before the first course hit the table, was probably just as well. Lana, sitting stiffly on the couch with her cocktail in her hand and an air hostess smile on her face while Alistair, 'all my friends call me Dash', told amusing anecdotes of his career as a scriptwriter, had a considerable amount of time in which to wonder what Joan really thought of her if this was the man Joan thought had been created solely with Lana in mind. For Dash, though not unattractive, was an ego on legs. Lana could imagine that when Dash first heard the news that God was dead it must have caused him a great deal of concern, pinching himself, running from mirror to mirror, walking up to people and saying hello just to see if they would say hello back. Dash had been everywhere, seen everything, and knew everyone. He had been lost in Alaska, had sailed across the Atlantic, explored Amazonia in a rubber dinghy, rescued a baby from a burning building, lived in Burma as a Buddhist monk, been married to a princess, been married to a junkie, had a limp from the injury he sustained saving the life of a young child during an earthquake in South America. Dash knew Marlon and George and Robert and Bette and Martin and Michael and Daryl and Liz and Jane. It was amazing, said Lana, that he seemed to know so much about all these people when he never stopped talking long enough to let anyone else get a word in about themselves. And yet you couldn't say he was as charming as a used condom. He was interesting. His life (when he lived it if not when he talked about it) was exciting. He was an inspired storyteller with an apparently limitless fund of incredible stories. 'I don't believe you,' Joan hissed at Lana in the kitchen. 'What do you mean you think he's boring? He's the most fascinating man I've ever met. For heaven's sake, Lana, this man's been out with Roseanna Arquette. He's gone partying with Madonna. He's got drunk with some of the most famous people in the world. Any woman in her right mind would give up going out for the next six years for just one date with Dash.' 'Fine,' said Lana. 'You let me stay here with Waldorf and you can go home with Dash.' 'Don't be ridiculous,' snapped Joan, thrusting the chocolate mousse into Lana's hands. 'If he seems a little overbearing it's probably just because he's nervous and shy. He knows you're here to meet him and he wants to make a good impression. Give him a chance.'

So Lana gave Dash a chance. When he offered to drive her home she smiled the way one does when the cat has done something clever and said, 'Oh, Dash, that would be wonderful. I can't thank you enough.' She gave him a chance and for fifteen minutes of the thirty-minute ride he told her about all the films he'd saved from being box office flops and/or critical disasters. 'People always want to know why I don't get into acting,' Dash said. 'Just last week Jeff Bridges wanted to know why I never thought of directing. But I guess I'm just one of those guys who likes to stay behind the scenes.' When they ran out of petrol, Dash was saying, 'I guess I've always been too modest for that sort of thing.' It was raining. The nearest service station was miles away. It was late and the road they were on was far from busy. They walked. Lana said she figured that even walking four miles in a storm with Dash talking about the time he was a rancher in Argentina was better than waiting in the car by herself on a lonely road, though it was by no means an easy decision. By the time they reached the station, Lana in her taffeta mini and strapless top and fun shawl was drenched. Her make-up was but a memory, her hair was flat and her shoes were peeling. Her legs were smooth but kind of blue. The night manager of the station offered her a pair of overalls and an old shirt he kept for emergencies. 'You look great,' he said when she came out of the back room, smiling at her in admiration. 'I always say that you can tell if a woman is really beautiful if she looks good in denim and flannel.' He gave her a towel to dry her hair. He told her a joke about a flat tyre that made her howl. He left her in charge of the station while he drove Dash back to the car with the petrol. He was the first to return. He tore into the station, jumped out of his car and ran into the office. 'Is that guy your husband?' he asked Lana. 'Are you kidding?' 'Your fiance?' 'No.' 'Your boyfriend?' 'I only just met him,' said Lana. 'We barely shook hands.' 'He sure talks a lot,' said her new friend. 'He sure does,' said Lana. 'Why don't you stay here till my shift's over and I'll drive you home?' And that was how Lana met Brian, the love of her life. They drank soda and played backgammon and told jokes till seven in the morning, and then Brian drove her home and a week later he moved in. 'I'll never be able to thank Joan enough,' says Lana today.

10

REAL WAYS OF MEETING MEN

Being astute, you will have noticed from the preceding chapter that the old-fashioned, traditional ways of meeting men are largely passive ones. True, you do have to be active enough to pick up the telephone or make it over to Martha May's for dinner on Wednesday, but aside from that they require very little personal initiative. They are merely part of the cause and effect relationship many of us have with life (you're in place a. when b. happens and because of that you become involved with c. – it looks like a plan, but it isn't. If you had been in d. when b. happened you would have wound up involved with y., and that would have looked like the plan). But now that system has broken down. We go to the dinners and the social gatherings we're invited to but we don't meet anyone. We drift gently along, blown by the breeze, and only years later discover that we're lost at sea.

'This is the new age,' says Jane. 'You can't leave these things to chance. If you really want to find a man you have to take an active part in the proceedings. The early bird catches the worm because she is out there in the garden, her tiny eyes sparkling, waiting for the little worm to poke its head up, not back in the nest practising her T'ai Chi. Be imaginative. Be resourceful. Go for the long shots. Remember that the more places you try the greater your chances of success.'

That all sounds like a lot of work to me.

'It is a lot of work, Serena,' says Jane. 'Don't you think you're worth it? Don't you think a lifetime of happiness with someone wonderful is worth a little effort on your part?'

Well, but I thought I was putting the work in when I was becoming the terrific person I am today. All the skills I've learned, the sharpness of my wit, my extensive knowledge of the detective novel, my ability to lace up knee-high boots with one hand in three seconds flat, my self-reliance, my independence, my familiarity with rawl plugs. What was all that for?

'To give you something to do while you were waiting to find the right man.'

But doesn't this all smack a bit of the old stereotype of the predatory female?

'It's a cold and calculating world,' says Jane. 'Do you think Bruce Springsteen got where he is today by staying in his room, playing his guitar, and then one day he looked out the window and there were 75,000 people in his mother's garden, all of them singing along with "The River"?'

'She makes sense to me,' you say. 'Just look where all this women's lib stuff has got us. I'm going to buy some new clothes, put auburn highlights in my hair, and have my nails done. Then what?'

Things to Do

Tired of waiting for the telephone to ring? Bored with playing Scrabble with the computer? Have you resorted to having your milk delivered so that a man comes to your door on a regular basis? Take heart. There are things you can do that will have you knee-deep in dates before you can say 'Lonely no more'.

Computer Dating

You're coming home from work on the tube. It's the
Friday night of a long, hard week. You're tired. It's
snowing outside. The tube is crowded and smells like
old laundry. You not only don't have a seat but have
nothing to hold on to so that every time the train stops,
starts, or makes a sudden turn you are flung against
other passengers. You think the man behind you in the
tweed overcoat may be taking an advantage. Oh how
you long to be home. And suddenly, right in front of
you, you see the photograph of a smiling couple,
heads just touching. 'You too can find love,' says the
advertisement. 'In over twenty years,' it continues,
'our introductions have been the start of many, many
thousands of love stories.' You lean forward so you
can read the smaller print, inadvertently belting the
woman sitting beneath the sign with your handbag.
'Oh, sorry,' you say, though distantly. It seems that
both Laurie and Bill led full lives, with many friends
and an astounding number of interests, but when Bill
was introduced to Laurie through Loveline he
immediately said to himself, 'Hallelujah! At last I've
found the woman I can really love.' 'Thank you,
Loveline, for bringing us together,' they say. 'Do you
want to meet someone with the same hopes, ambitions
and interests as yourself?' asks the ad. Yeah, you
think, I would. 'Wouldn't you like somebody to love?' I
sure would, you say to yourself, unaware that your
lips are moving. You don't much like the look of Bill
(he's a soup slurper if ever you saw one), but Laurie,
wearing the same smile as the woman who has lost ten
stone in two months without dieting, does seem pretty
fond of him. Yes, you think to yourself, it's simple. I fill
out the form, they put it through their computer, they
come up with half a dozen men who are warmhearted,
hate wine bars, and feel ambivalent towards children,
just like me, and all I have to do is meet them. What
could be easier or more logical?

Jane says that nothing is easier or more logical. I say the same thing that my Aunt Beryl said to the waiter who assured her that the salmon was fresh that morning: ha.

I'm sure that Laurie and Bill, and Mavis and Arthur, and Jude and Kevin, and all the other smiling couples who have found each other through the miracle of electronics are as happy together as a hot dog and its roll. But when you look at their photograph, he in his pastel pullover and she in her good white blouse and pearls, there are several questions you should be asking yourself besides 'If it worked for them why shouldn't it work for me?' You should be asking yourself why all these couples look as though they've already been married to each other for at least fifteen years. You should be asking yourself how many years Laurie belonged to Loveline; how many dates she had to endure with shy, warmhearted men who liked musical comedies and sheep, how many suppers in Pizza Express, how many bloody walks in the rain, up to her ankles in mud and sheep poo while he hummed the entire score of *Oklahoma!* and she caught the flu, before she met Bill. You should be asking yourself what sort of people would let their feelings for one another be used as a crass commercial tool. It's bad enough that we've got Michael Jackson selling us Pepsi, but the thought of normal, ordinary people selling us love is the sort of thing that makes a person feel cynical about human nature.

'Serena,' says Jane, 'you have a streak of conservatism in you that would make Mrs Thatcher seem radical. There is nothing wrong with a system that is dedicated to bringing together like-minded people. There is nothing wrong with wanting to shout your love from the highest mountaintop. Stop being such a drag.'

And you might also keep in mind the fact that compatibility has precious little to do with love. Just because you and Jim both enjoy parties (both you and Jim have a character failing here), like popular music and going to the cinema, are fond of horses and infants and wouldn't eat anything with a cream sauce on it, it unfortunately doesn't mean that when he smiles at you your heart's going to end up in your toes.

Love is not only the enemy of sleep, sanity and rational behaviour, it is the enemy of logic as well. You cannot use the same criteria for losing your heart that you use for finding a flatmate or someone to go on holiday with. One of the happiest couples I know are David and Pat. They have so little in common that just the fact that they ever met has been used by some as proof of God.

He is quiet, serious, conservative and shy. She is loud, fun-loving, extrovert and flamboyant. He hates crowds. She thinks life is a party. He is never publicly demonstrative of his affections, she is always grabbing him in the street. She likes to go out dancing, he'd rather stay home and watch television while he flosses his teeth. Smart money would have given them about three weeks together before they drove each other out of their minds. And yet, years later, here they are, still together and still in love. She makes his life exciting. He gives her life stability. If they had filled out the Loveline application form they would never have met. He would have been matched with some meat-eating stockbroker whose idea of fun was a dinner at which everyone talked about the price of pork rinds, and she would have been matched with a drop-out sitar player who lived on sunflower seeds and enjoyed astral projection.

The Personals
The popularity of the personal ad, like that of bottled water, has skyrocketed in the past decade or so. Whereas not so very long ago most of us could have lived a long and full life without ever meeting anyone

who had placed or answered a personal ad, now it is just as likely that we will know a personal person as it is that we will know an ex-smoker. They're all over the place. Slowly and unobtrusively, turn to the person next to you, glance over at the person across the way, look behind you at the girl wearing the straw hat and the Elvis Is Alive button. Statistics show that at least one of those people, or maybe all of them, have searched for love and romance among the lonely hearts in the past eighteen months. You're staggered, right? You say, 'Wow!' Even that heart-crushing redhead at work, Mona of the tight skirts and temptress smile, has answered four or five in her time.

There are several prominent theories afoot to explain the popularity of the personal ad. Like a mountain or a killer waterfall, they are there. People have a tendency to believe everything they read. 'Of course Freddie Starr ate that girl's hamster,' they say. 'I read it in the paper, didn't I?' Modern living, as we have already discovered, makes it difficult for people to meet. The more something is done the more people want to do it. 'Well, all those neat-sounding people are taking out ads,' you say to yourself. 'There must be something to them after all.' And people like to gamble. A species that can convince itself that no matter how much death, insanity, mayhem and destruction it causes God will always save it in the end likes to live on hope.

So what are the personals all about? 'They are,' says Jane, 'like computer dating, one way of making contact with people you would otherwise never have the opportunity of meeting. I can't tell you the number of really nice men I have met through the ads.'

Lonesome me seeks lonesome you for long duet. Tall, good-looking guy with great sense of humour and small yacht would like to meet petite, attractive brunette who would make his crêpes suzette. Attractive, independent, multi-lingual professional woman who likes opera, gourmet dining, walking in

the rain and travel would like to meet similar man
whose first language is love. Gorgeous blonde with
plenty of personality and pizazz sought by handsome
Porsche driver who is tired of looking to buy and
winding up with sub-lets. Divorced doctor who loves
sailing, classical music, good food, great books and
walking in the rain would like to try again with terrific
woman, 25-35, who isn't into game playing, please
send photo. I'm not the sort of person who would ever
place or answer a personal ad. Are you? Sincere,
sensitive male with good job and own home, looking
to settle down with woman more interested in
kindness and devotion than cheap thrills. Creative,
sunny, compassionate woman who is great company
and a mean cherry cheesecake baker wants like man
for long-term relationship.

'Sounds all right to me,' you say.

And, yes, I guess they do. You have noted, of course,
that none of these people sounds really lonely. That
none of these people gives the impression of being
desperate. That all of these people sound pretty
wonderful. No boring file clerks whose hobby is
sending away for the free brochures in the Sunday
magazines here. No neurotics who sleep with baseball
bats under their pillows or count to twelve before they
enter any room in this bunch. No one with short legs
or pot bellies or less hair than they had when they
came into this world. No one who is insensitive or
insincere; no one who is cranky in the morning or who
couldn't tell the truth if his life depended on it; no one
who loves Rambo or wouldn't go out in the rain if you
offered to transport him in a tank.

'You mean,' you say, that little rise of horror in your
voice, 'you mean you think people lie?'

No, of course not. Though, as my mother has always
been quick to point out, not lying is not precisely the
same as telling the truth. But even if you knew the
truth about yourself you would be unlikely to put it in

an ad that you hoped some nice, likeable person was going to answer. The woman who writes: Average-looking woman with lived-in body and so many grey hairs that when she looks in the mirror she thinks it must be snowing, seeks sweet, kind caring man to give her love and affection and not mind her frequent depressions, her dislike of animals, and her bouts of being disinterested in sex. If I have to eat one more frozen dinner with a candle stuck in the gin bottle to make me think I'm not alone I may do something drastic like join the Barry Manilow fan club. Who will save me from this fate worse than death? might as well send in her membership fee right away, because the number of handsome, professional men with a great sense of humour and their own jets who are going to be replying are few. No person with any sense is going to answer an ad that says: Unattractive but interesting looking and sloppy art teacher who is always borrowing money from his friends and who goes nuts if anybody touches his things, looking for an attractive, funny woman who knows how to cook.

'My friend Martina met her husband through the personal ads,' says Jane. 'He was an urban cowboy with the heart of a country boy looking for a girl to remind him of his roots and plant some new ones. Remember him?'

I remember Zebra-man.

'Who?'

Exactly.

My friend Liza, like the rest of us, was not the sort of person to resort to personal advertising. But one Sunday morning she was reading through the papers when this ad caught her eye:

> Women find me sympathetic and attractive. Men find me intelligent and reliable. My mother thinks I'm great. I have everything I want – friends,

money, a good job, a terrific life –
except for that special someone. I am
looking for a woman who will share
my love of rock-and-roll, Tom Wolfe
and deep-fried artichoke hearts, as
well as my love of the world's wildlife.

Oh boy, thought Liza. Here he is. Without a second
thought Liza penned her reply and enclosed a picture
of herself looking ravishing holding a fox cub whose
life she'd saved. Two days later he telephoned. His
voice was rich and deep and warmly humorous. He
wondered if her legs were really as long as they
appeared in the photograph or if she'd been standing
on something.

They met. He was a little short for Liza, but so is
Bruce Springsteen, so she didn't let that bother her,
especially as he was both cute and charming. He really
did have an interesting job, lots of friends, a good life
and a mother who thought he was the best thing since
indoor plumbing. Liza and he went to the movies.
They went out to dinner. They went dancing. Her
blood wasn't flashing like a neon sign or anything, but
she did like him. She never once found herself
thinking, is he a little too neat? a little too
well-organized? does his laugh have a hysterical edge
to it? could this man be a psychopath disguised as a
lover of whales? He seemed worth getting to know. He
finally invited her over for dinner one night. 'I'll make
the tamales and you bring the wine,' he said. Liza said
'Ole!'

'Where do the zebras come in?'

We're getting to them. Be patient.

All this time, though there had been a certain
amount of random sympathy expressed for several
endangered species there had been no real heavy sell
on the wildlife front. So Liza was relaxed. In her
experience, people who are actively concerned that the

planet's animal population is dropping at an alarming
rate tend to turn into conservation bores with little
provocation. You say, 'Oh, the poor otters,' and three
hours later he's still reeling off the statistics and
describing the death throes. But with Abe (that was his
name) there was no such thing. He could pass a pet
store without becoming emotional. He could say 'zoo'
and 'safari park' without becoming apoplectic. He
didn't start going on about the dolphins every time
you ordered tuna salad. Only once, when she asked
him what his favourite animal was, did his eyes get
kind of misty as he said, 'Zebras.'

The night of the dinner arrived. Liza decided to be
understated in a pair of chinos and a denim work shirt.
She put her hair up in case he wanted to take it down
later. She liberally doused herself from her special
cache of Poison. She rang the bell.

Here is what happened next in Liza's own words:
'He met me at the door and gave me a little
neighbourly peck on the cheek. I could hear Bob
Seger singing from the living room (not really Bob
Seger, Serena, on a record). I sort of half-noticed, you
know, that there were a lot of pictures of zebras on the
walls of the hall, but I didn't think anything of it. I
didn't even notice that the carpet was patterned to
look like zebra skin. I followed him into the kitchen.
The floor was black and white tiles, just like my
mother's, but I was a little surprised to see that he had
painted all the appliances to look like zebras. The
cabinets were green. The tablecloth was covered with
tiny zebras, looking thoughtful. "Oh, isn't that
adorable," I said. He said, "Wait'll you see the
bathroom." So I trotted off to see the bathroom. He'd
painted this amazing mural of zebras at a watering
hole all over the walls. The bath mat, toilet seat cover
and towels were all zebra print. Zebras clutched the
loo paper. A zebra held the toothbrushes. There was
an inflatable zebra in the tub instead of ducks. I mean,

come on, Serena, most people do have ducks, don't they? I went back to the kitchen, where there was a plate of these really great nachos on the table and a glass of wine waiting for me. I felt better about the bathroom. "Boy," I said, "you really do like zebras." He said he did. "Shall we take our drinks into the living room?" he asked. I, like a dope, said, "Sure."

'I really don't know if I can describe the living room and do it justice. It was sort of a cross between a Victorian hunting lodge and a theme park. Everything in the living room was zebra. The couch, the chairs, the walls, even the lampshades. There was even a zebra head over the mantelpiece. But that wasn't the worst, Serena. Not by a long shot. The worst thing was that there were zebras everywhere. Little zebras, big zebras, middle-sized zebras. Zebras made out of plastic and zebras made out of papier mache and zebras made out of wood. Bronze zebras and ebony zebras and this zebra that must have been on a carousel once. There was even a chess set on the coffee table whose pieces were zebras.' [Here I interrupted to ask, 'What did you say to him?'] 'Well, I sat down on this chair that was covered so it looked like a zebra head and I said, "Gee, I guess you're pretty easy to buy Christmas presents for." And then I told him that I'd suddenly gotten my period and my cramps were killing me and I didn't have anything with me and I was afraid of bleeding all over the animals, and I went home.'

And I rest my case.

Places to Go

Perhaps you have put in several personal ads and had no answers. Perhaps you have answered several personal ads, and though they led to a bottle of house red at a nearby winebar they did not lead to love. Maybe it's begun to worry you that all the men the dating agency turns up bear a striking physical resemblance to one another and smell like mouthwash. Maybe you've begun toying with the idea of lying on the Loveline ad to make the computer think that you're a twenty-year-old silver-blonde model who loves dancing and physical-contact sports and men who are extroverted and into power. 'Well, hey,' you say. 'I've done what I could. I guess it's all-alone-by-the-telephone time once more.'

'Not a bit of it,' says Jane. 'You haven't even begun yet.'

'I haven't?' you ask.

'No. The motto of any woman who is serious about finding a man in these days of scarcity and deprivation has got to be: As long as there is one single, heterosexual man left on this planet I will not rest until I've found him.'

'It is?'

'You bet your battery-operated vibrator with the attachable heads it is.'

Now that you know that you haven't begun yet, you're probably wondering what – aside from putting a For Sale sign across your chest and marching up and down the high street – there could possibly be left to do. A few years back, the answer would have been 'nothing', but nowadays the possibilities are almost endless. If Mr Right won't come to you, then you must go to seek him out in the places where he is most likely to be. 'Yes,' says Jane, 'this is calculated. Leave nothing to chance – chance is fickle and unreliable.' You may never be able to walk into a supermarket for a box of macaroni with a light heart again, but Jane guarantees that her method will eventually lead to rigatoni for two.

Of course, when embarking upon serious man-hunting, a person must always look her best. Every minute of the day. Even when you are not actively seeking him out, you must allow for the possibility that you might run into him by accident. This means that a person can never afford to leave the house looking anything less than impeccable and alluring. No dashing around the corner for a container of milk with a raincoat over your pyjamas. No running out with the rubbish with the curlers still in your hair. No thinking, it's only the man for the boiler. If the man for the boiler isn't himself single, well-built and fond of parrots, he may have a partner who is. This means that you do not slouch over to the supermarket in your old paint-spattered jeans and a baggy sweater, your hair pinned up with a My Little Pony clip. That if you have to take the cat to the vet you make sure you're wearing something sexy, whether or not Moggy becomes incontinent in crowds. There can be no time when you relax your vigilance. No situation where you lower your standards. No 'five minutes' when you leave the house with a naked face and a scarf over your head. 'You have to think like a Girl Guide,' says Jane. 'Always be prepared.'

Jane Fforbes-Smythe's List of Places to Frequent in Search of Men

Pubs

'You what?' you gasp. 'Have you ever noticed the men who hang out in pubs? Do you know what happens to a woman who walks into a pub on her own?'

As a matter of fact, I have. Half the men still sober enough to see start grimacing at one another and undressing her with their eyes, and the other half blow smoke in her face. And yet Jane is right, pubs are definitely places where men hang out. They meet each other there after work to unwind. If they don't go to work, they meet each other there to unwind. They go there by themselves when they're lonely or have had a hard day or are in a bad mood or can't face going home

ALWAYS BE PREPARED.

with a take-away. Men like pubs. They are dark and smoky and noisy, often have games you can play when the conversation drags, and you can behave like an idiot in a pub and no one will say much more than, 'Oh, don't mind Jimmy, he always gets like that after twenty-three beers.'

'You shouldn't assume, Serena,' says Jane, 'that just because a man is in a pub that he is drinking. Men go into pubs for society and companionship and to engage in intellectually stimulating debate. Pubs these days sell mineral water and fruit juice and non-alcoholic wine and beer.'

My mother and I remain unconvinced. 'Your Uncle Joe used to hang out in pubs,' my mother reminisces, 'and that was because he was a drunk.' And I would have to add that all the men I have known who frequented pubs with any regularity or sense of purpose have done so not because they were interested in meeting some charming woman anxious for a vigorous discussion of monetarism, but because they wanted to get pissed as a newt, or, in the old days, because they were hoping to get laid.

'In the course I took on finding a husband, they told you what to do when you go into a pub by yourself,' says Jane. 'You walk in, you order yourself a Perrier with ice and lemon, and when some nice chap comes up to you and says, "What's a fascinating woman like yourself doing in an establishment like this?" you say, "I'm looking for someone to love. What are you doing here?" '

If you are determined to hang out in pubs, then you should pick your pubs pretty carefully. Pubs near law courts and hospitals make sense. Pubs near newspaper offices do not make sense. Pubs in hotels and tourist areas are definitely dodgy. People remembering that scene in *My Sister Eileen* where half the Brazilian navy follow Eileen home might be tempted to try pubs near docks, but you should never take too lightly all the warnings your mother gave you about sailors. Neighbourhood pubs (unless the neighbourhood is Knightsbridge or Beverly Hills, perhaps) are often populated by people who aren't sure what day it is, never mind being intrigued to learn that you've come into the Prince of Wales (Dart Tournament Every Friday Night) looking for love.

In most cases, I'd say that your best bet would be to show some interest in the barman. Not only is he likely to be the one person in the place who is sober, he's also the only one who has a really good reason for being there.

Hardware Shops
Now that most pubs and clubs have been opened to women, real hardware shops (not the kind that sell

flan dishes and tea kettles, the kind that sell ballpeen hammers, loose screws and nails, hard-hats with lights on them and all sorts of odd-looking metal bits and bobs), plumbing supply stores and lumber yards (not to be confused with DIY centres) are almost the only places (with the exception of the hunting lodge, the duck blind and a surprisingly large number of executive lavatories) that are almost exclusively male preserves.

'Hardware shops are perfect', says Jane. 'Not only are there never any other women in them, and not only do the displays of saw blades and copper tubing tend to show a person off to good advantage, but it gives you a chance to ask for help and advice. Men love giving help and advice.'

The problem with this one is subtle. If you go in as yourself in your lurex cycling pants and matching top, mumbling something about needing a thingy for a whatsit, you're likely to be about as welcome as a cocktail waitress suddenly showing up in the ring during the middle of the crucial seventh round. All the builders, plumbers, house painters, contractors, etc. want to do is get on with their jobs. At eleven o'clock on a Monday morning when there's sewage all over Mrs Hulahan's kitchen or he accidentally ran over his tool bag backing out of the drive, the last thing a man wants is some woman smiling at him sweetly and wanting to know what size nail she needs to put up a shelf. The man behind the counter will be rude to you (civility is never in their contracts) and the harried customers, their trucks double-parked and their clients hysterical, will cut in front of you, assuming that you've only wandered in for directions. If, on the other hand, you dress sensibly and seriously in your old jeans and lumberjack shirt, they will not only take you for one of the boys, they will expect you to know the difference between a wing nut and a woodscrew as well.

The problem with turning up in unexpected places is that men, unlike women, can only concentrate on one thing at a time. Your father would go to work and do his job and then he would come home and he would mow the lawn or read the paper or watch television or open the jar of pickled onions that your mother couldn't budge. But your mother would spend the day doing the household chores, solving her sister's marital problems, making you that pleated skirt you couldn't live without, amusing the baby, fixing supper, organizing the hospital flower show, doing all your father's errands, going to the shops for the loaf of bread, two pints of milk and tin of beans she knew she would need tomorrow (but would not be able to get tomorrow, because tomorrow she had the cub scouts, a sit-down dinner for twenty and the school outing to get together), and while your father was recovering from his heavy day, she'd be thickening the stew, quizzing you on your spelling words, and feeding the dog. When she asked your father if he'd mind getting the tin of apple sauce for her from the top shelf, he'd say, 'For heaven's sake, honey, I'm opening the onions. I only have one pair of hands, you know. I can't do two things at a time.' So it is that a woman who is catering the Summit Conference lunch and has run into the supermarket for a few last-minute items will pull herself together if she sees this Tom Selleck look-alike reading the labels on the dairy spreads and looking confused, and will offer him assistance. But a man whose mind is on sheetrock will not even notice the beautiful and intelligent woman staring wistfully at the rawl plugs. Even if she were naked it wouldn't be until he got back outside, into the van, and was pulling away from the kerb that he would say to himself, 'Gee, she must be cold. I wonder if I should have got another pound of nails while I was there, just in case.'

Racetracks

'Racetracks?' I asked. 'Jane, are you serious? The only men who hang out at racetracks are multimillionaires with a sudden desire to drink champagne outdoors with their new mistress or guys whose wives think they're at work and not about to put the family savings down on Crazy Monday's nose.'

She's serious. 'It's much better than the betting shops,' she maintains, 'because you don't have to fight your way past the drunks and vagrants to get inside and racetracks aren't so smoky.'

Well, yes, they do have those things going for them.

'And there are always a lot of men around.'

There are a lot of horses, too. And, like the horses, the men who are around are likely to be a little single-minded.

'No,' says Jane, 'it's absolutely perfect. If they've just lost their shirts they head for the bar and are delighted to have some attractive woman come along to cheer them up. Whereas, if they've just won they head for the bar and are looking for some gorgeous girl to help them celebrate.'

I don't know, I argued. It seems to me that the chaps a person is likely to encounter at a racetrack are just the sort to sell the silver service so they can bet on a sure thing. Aren't gamblers prone to the sort of compulsive behaviour our mothers always warned us about?

'Not everybody at a racetrack is a candidate for gamblers anonymous, you know,' said Jane. 'Racing is a sport.'

So is dog fighting.

'Racing was the sport of kings,' persisted Jane.

And armed aggression was what they did after they'd relaxed at the track.

Sports Events

In the great tradition of the racetrack are all the other spectator sports (I have refused to allow snooker or darts) that Jane can think of.

'But Jane,' I said, 'not only are many sports distastefully violent and one or two of them actually activities in which people have died, most of them are either the sort of things men go to with like-minded girlfriends or important occasions for male bonding.'

A man goes to boxing matches with women who find bruises sexy and the sound of bones being crushed titillating, with women who shout out, 'That's it, Killer, stomp on him, stomp on him,' not in the hope that he's going to sit next to someone who keeps her eyes closed through the bloody bits and wants to know if he thinks the guy in the white trunks is really hurt.

A man doesn't go to a football game expecting to meet the love of his life but to find someone whose face he can grind into the ground.

Jane, however, has learned nothing from her marriage course if not to be philosophical. 'You never know who you're going to run into while you're buying a hamburger or a bag of crisps,' she says.

The Incredible Hulk. Giant Haystacks. Some guy who can't remember his own name unless he looks in his wallet. Men with little crocodiles on their shirts.

'That shows how much you know,' says Jane. 'I once ran into Eric Clapton at Wimbledon.'

And?

'And he was very nice. He let me hold his drink while he signed my programme.'

Well, to be fair, I did once run into Enrico, the third great love of my life, while waiting in the beer queue at the Harrow Bowling Tournament.

'And what happened? Did he sweep you up into his arms? Did he tell you how much he'd missed you? Did he beg you to come back?'

He reminded me that I still had his Jim Kweskin album and introduced me to his wife.

Sports fans are a tricky bunch. On the one hand they get very tetchy very fast if they're distracted from the most brilliant goal of the season by someone tugging on their sleeve wanting to know what's happening and who's got the ball. On the other hand, they're not always best pleased to find themselves sitting next to some cute blonde with dimples who turns out to know more about the game, its history, its rules, its play, and the records of the players on the field than they do. You have to know enough so that you won't be bored out of your brain when it becomes apparent that he has nothing to talk about other than the many, many games he's seen, how they compare with one another, and why most referees have the brains and eyesight of a cork, and not so much that he feels you're challenging his authority. For even several years out of the Stone Age, as we apparently are, men like to think that there are certain areas where they are dominant. They are willing to give women clothes (except for *haute couture*), food (except for *haute cuisine*), and children and childbearing (practical, not theoretical), but they draw the line at sports, business, killing and bartending.

'As usual, Serena,' says Jane, 'you've missed out an important bit.'

'Oh?'

'The only men you might meet at a sports event aren't the fans you know. What about the sportsmen themselves?'

You mean boxers? Hockey players? Golfers? Wrestlers? Jane, have you ever had lunch with a hockey player? Do you know what it's like sitting across from someone who has no teeth? Have you ever tried to discuss anything really complicated with a boxer? Do you think a man who spends all his spare time hitting a little ball around the lawn is going to have a lot of interesting conversation? Do you think a man who has his head pounded on the ground and his legs bent behind his neck every Thursday is going to be a lot of fun in bed?

Nor do sportsmen age very well. Their lean, trim bodies and rippling muscles may make your heart skip a few beats when they're in their prime. But just wait a few years. The lean begins to thicken. The trim begins to spread. The muscle turns to fat. They get arthritis and rheumatism, or their backs give out, or they get to the middle of a sentence and forget what they were saying. Sometimes, unable to cope with the loss of their glory days, they become dependent on a bottle or two of gin a day, pitiful creatures waiting to waylay each new customer in the pub with the story of the year the Queen sent them a fan letter. They suffer a tragic crash at what was meant to be their last race.

'Oh yeah?' sneers Jane. 'And what about Ali Kahn? I seem to remember you thinking he was pretty cute. And Daley Thompson? You wouldn't want to help him stay in shape?'

There are exceptions to every rule.

Service Stations and Garages

Ever since the night Jane and I couldn't get the new petrol cap off at the service station I have seen the wisdom of this piece of advice. (The reason I couldn't get the cap off was because the garage where the car had gone for repairs had lost the keys – an event that had never happened before in the long history of Marty's Motors – and there had been no spare for the petrol cap. I had stood shoulder to shoulder with Marty while he explained the working of the new cap to me, but the honest truth is that I probably wasn't paying as much attention as I should have been. I was saying, 'Yeah, sure, right, of course I understand,' but I was concentrating more on the gold specks in his warm brown eyes than I was on which direction to turn the key. I have always been a sucker for men who work with their hands.) Anyway, the moment of reckoning comes when Jane and I, returning from an evening at the airport (where Jane had said our chances of meeting a couple of local, unwed businessmen whose flights had been delayed were excellent because of the snow), stop for petrol, and I can't get the cap off. The first man who tried to help us said, 'I hope you don't have far to go. I could give you a lift if you want.' The second man said, 'Why don't I give your friend a lift home.' The third got taken out for a celebratory coffee.

In fact, I would have to admit that I have met more men through my car than I have through Jane. They appear out of nowhere to give you a push. They are cheerful about helping you figure out the intricacies of the air pump. They like to give you advice on motor oil and tyres. They love to lean over the engine and say things like, 'Uhoh, that doesn't sound too good.'

My friend Judy met her husband the night her clutch cable snapped on a hill in the rain. He's an AA repairman. 'I mean,' Judy told me later, 'you'd be happy enough if Alice Cooper turned up in that little yellow truck with the flashing light under those circumstances. Here I was soaking wet and nervous and wondering if I was ever going to get home, and along comes this absolute sweetiepie who didn't get upset that I was crying and couldn't understand his instructions about being towed, who hummed 'Racing in the Streets' while he hooked up the pole, and who stopped twice on the way to see if I was all right. I mean, I had to invite him in for a cup of tea, didn't I?'

Stick to used cars, though. Their lives are more eventful.

Supermarkets
Jane's reasoning on supermarkets as a likely setting for a meeting that might eventually lead to your having a reason for having a double bed that is acceptable to your mother is that 'everybody has to eat'. And so they do.

'Single men with broad backs and well-developed

chest muscles are part of everybody,' says Jane.
'Supermarkets sell food. Ergo, single men with broad
backs and well-developed chest muscles will be found
in supermarkets.'

To which one can only raise a quizzical eyebrow and
smile thinly. For Jane's argument is, in fact, a classic
example of what we philosophers call a sophism. It
looks logical. A + B = C. But things are not always as
they seem. Jane's argument is similar to saying that
whales are to be found in water, the lake near my
house is water, therefore I will go to the lake to see a
whale. Whales do not usually hang out in lakes (where
there is little room for them to splash around and they
are in danger of being hit by small, remote-controlled
sailing vessels). Likewise, desirable, unattached men
with good physiques do not normally frequent aisle 3,

canned vegetables, soups, sauces, and dried beans (where there is little room for them to splash around and they are in danger of being hit by elderly ladies who can't reach the top shelf and small children with chocolate on their hands). Single men do not need to frequent supermarkets because they are, by definition, unneedy of shopping trolleys filled with sides of beef and bags of potatoes. Single men are fed by their mothers, their friends, their female admirers, and Tony's Pleasing Pizzas. If a single man feels like having lentil soup for supper he will stop at the corner store and pick it up with the milk and the cat food. If he needs bread he will stop at the bakery, and so forth. So a person who puts on her best silver shoes and her leather dress, swabs down her face with micro-targeted skin gel, applies a painter's palette to her eyes, and douses herself with Opium, all to stand by the freezer case with a puzzled frown on her beautiful face so that she can accost the first broad-backed, rippling of chest single man she sees pushing his trolley towards her whether he thinks there is an enormous difference between petit pois and minted garden fresh peas is heading for a fall. Any man seen thus, especially if he is peering at a handwritten shopping list as he walks along, is either married or gay. And the chances are that less than half an aisle behind him there is some guy saying, 'I am not going to stand by and let you put that muck in your stomach. If you want baked beans I'll make them myself,' or some wan-looking woman with two small children hanging off her and a ten-pound box of soap powder in her arms calling, 'Henry, Henry, did you say you wanted spaghetti or those little things that look like shells?'

Carparks
Jane claims that the beauty of the carpark as a meeting place is self-evident. 'Everything else has its

drawbacks,' says Jane. 'But not the carpark. It's almost as though God said to Himself, "What can I give the single people of the world as a special little present, something just for them?" And then all of a sudden there was a flash of lightning, and He snapped his fingers and shouted, "I've got it! I'll give them the carpark!" '

For you see, although a person who has put on her tightest jeans and most flattering electric-blue sweater to buy five pounds of six-inch nails or watch two grown men try to beat each other's brains out might look a little overly fashion conscious and out of place; and though a person who wears her form-flattering jersey suit and those little black shoes with the bows down the front to run around the park or bring the car in for its service might seem a little over-dressed, a person can wear anything in a carpark. Shorts, formal gowns, sportswear, business suits, afternoon dresses, denim shirts, cashmere sweaters – you name it and the carpark will accept it without a blink.

You can also wander around a carpark for a very long time before anyone will think you're trying to steal something or planting a bomb. How long, on the other hand, can you make your grocery shopping last? A half hour? An hour? Two hours? Eventually someone will notice that you've been past the meat case fourteen times and the manager will be called. 'Are you intending to buy something, madam,' he will ask, 'or are you trying to commit the prices to memory?' A carpark holds no such problems. You can roam its perimeters for hours. You can go off for a coffee or a quick cheese croissant and come back refreshed to start again. If the weather is nice, you can sit on a bumper and read the paper, just as though you are waiting for someone to come with your keys.

'But the real beauty,' says Jane, 'is that instead of being limited to "Excuse me, but I think that's my seat", or "I'm sorry but I was here first", or "Is it true the dairy herds have been infected with a highly contagious virus?" or "Would you mind if I just held this up against you for a moment? I think you're almost my father's size", you can start off the way you would like things to end.'

'Like what?'

'For instance, you could say, "Oh, I'm really sorry to bother you, but I've dropped my keys under that car, and well, and, you know, this is sort of embarrassing, but because of this incredibly short skirt I'm wearing I can't really bend down to get them myself. Do you think you could help?" Or you could say, "Oh, thank you, thank you so much," as he takes the three carrier bags and the rubber plant out of your hands. "My car's just over there. It's my flatmate's birthday and I'm trying to organize the surprise party for her. I just didn't realize how heavy all this stuff was. I don't know what I would have done if you hadn't come along. My goodness but you're strong. How can I ever thank you? Are you busy tonight? Would you like to come along?" There's really nothing to it.'

What I would like to know is just how long she had to stagger around the car park with three carrier bags of shopping and a four-foot high rubber plant before some hero offered to help her.

Entertainments

Even I cannot argue with the fact that, with the exception of a few recluses, most people do regularly leave their homes in search of entertainment of one sort or another. They go to the cinema, to the theatre, to concerts, to the ballet and to the opera. According to the Fforbes-Smythe Law of Probability, out there, where the bright lights beckon, are thousands of men looking for a good time or a little culture – and someone with whom to share it.

'A woman,' says Jane, 'should never be shy or afraid of going places on her own. How are you ever going to meet someone if you spend all your evenings at home, talking to the television and trying not to go off your diet? Going out by yourself has three major advantages: 1. it gives you a real excuse (not that you should need one) to put those blond highlights in your hair and wear something excessive; 2. it puts you, looking wonderful, in the path of countless eligible men; 3. even if you don't meet anyone you get to see the show.'

And she does have a point. Why should a person miss seeing Dustin Hoffman in *Death of a Salesman* just because she has no one to go to the cinema with her? There you are on a Saturday night after a long and demanding week, in need of a little relaxation, but all your friends are busy (the married ones are in some public place arguing with their husbands and the single ones are moving, like grazing cattle across the plains, from one late-night supermarket to the next). So what do you do? Head for the tortilla chips, the bean dip and the gin? Think, well that's terrific, really, I'll be able to do at least another square inch on my tapestry tonight. Or do you say to yourself, heck, nothing would cheer me up more than to spend two hours in the dark looking at Jeff Bridges, I think I'll go to the cinema? Do you say to yourself, well golly, it's been about fourteen years since I last saw *Swan Lake*, I rather fancy seeing if they've changed it at all since then? If you have any sense you will make yourself presentable, kiss the parrot, turn off all the lights but the one you leave on to fool the burglars, double-lock the door, and steam out on the town. What law says you can't have a good time on your own? Is a concert less enjoyable because there is no man beside you to comment on the bowing of the first violin? Is a stroll through the museum less pleasurable because there is no man standing in front of you, blocking your view as he explains what the three red squares and the splash of yellow in the corner mean? Would a play lose its power if the man sleeping gently beside you wasn't actually yours? Do you say to yourself, 'Yeah, but what's the fun of going to watch a three-hour Japanese film if there's no one to tell me later that I must be an imbecile if I didn't understand that it was a metaphor for the modern world?'

Go, I say, go go go – and have a good time. But don't expect to find a clutch of princes queueing up for pop corn or a quick brandy. Most of the princes you will find out and about, being entertained, will be with their princesses.

'But not all of them,' says Jane. 'At least one of them will have had a fight with his princess just before curtain time and will be on his own, wondering what he sees in the selfish bitch. At least one of them will be a visitor. At least one of them will be recently divorced and determined not to stay home alone, where the temptation to call up his ex-wife just to hear another voice, even one that is raised in anger, is so great. At least one of them will be an aficionado of the Bulgarian opera who always goes on his own.'

Maybe, but I can't help thinking that the only form of entertainment at which one is likely to find any reasonable number of single, unaccompanied men is a striptease.

'What about Jenny?' asks Jane. 'Huh? What about her?'

It is true that my friend Jenny once met a very cute window cleaner at a Pink Floyd concert. He'd been caught at the door trying to smuggle in a bottle of wine and was given the option of drinking it right then and there or seeing it go to the bouncer. So he drank it then and there. This developed into a conversation starter when he sat on Jenny by mistake as he was trying to get to his seat, as you can imagine it might. Soon they were sharing her bottle of tequila, and at the end of the evening (as unlikely as it seems) he walked her home.

But I can't help thinking that that was a fluke. Just

one of those things. Someone's going to win the pools, and someone's going to be picked off the street and turned into an international star, and someone's going to go to a rock concert and be noticed by the lead guitarist and invited back stage for a drink afterwards – but the chances are that it isn't going to be you. I myself have been to quite a few rock concerts in my time, and though I have often interacted with the people near me ('Do you think you could blow the smoke the other way?', 'I'm sorry, is Mr Springsteen's singing interfering with your conversation?', 'How very thoughtful of you to vomit in that brown bag'), I have never actually met anyone I thought I might like to see again. If you do see someone you might possibly consider meeting again in a less crowded venue, he is usually with someone else or banging away on the drums. I have also been to any number of films, plays, concerts, recitals, and, once, deranged by a heavy infatuation, an opera, but I have never fallen in love, nor been fallen in love with, during the intermission.

And let's just say, for the sake of argument, that you are sitting there, all comfortable and relaxed and looking forward to an evening of medieval chamber music, when all of a sudden a deep and sensationally sensuous voice says, 'Pardon me, but could you move your coat? I believe that's my seat,' and you look up from your perusal of the programme to find yourself staring into the face of the prince of your dreams. Unable, in the first flush of lust surprised, actually to formulate a sentence as long as, 'Oh, I'm so sorry', you nod. You bundle your coat onto your lap, grinning at him like someone who wants to sell him something (which I suppose you do). You wish that you had listened to Jane and made a routine of plucking your eyebrows and curling your lashes. You wish you had worn something that would hint at the fact that you do have breasts. The lights dim. The musicians take their places. They begin to play. Unless a fire breaks out, the musicians will play until the end of the concert, giving you little opportunity to regain your voice and strike up a conversation.

Parks and Playgrounds

Years ago, when the divorce rate was down and exercise was what you got when you walked to the office instead of taking the bus, the only men you were likely to find in parks or playgrounds were with their families, or lurking behind a bush waiting to expose themselves or strangle passing secretaries. Nowadays, however, the parks and playgrounds of the Western world are apparently filled to bursting with single fathers trying to think of something to do with the kids between lunch and supper on their weekend to have them. And competing with the single fathers for space are the thousands of corporate executives and criminal lawyers out jogging or running, the committed cyclists, the devoted dog-owners, and the occasional martial arts show-off.

'What could be easier?' asks Jane. 'Just put on your best silk boxer shorts, pack up a nice lunch and a bottle of wine, and head into the great outdoors. Fresh air, sunshine, and a relaxed and natural atmosphere.'

Being out of doors makes people feel free and easy. There is a spontaneous camaraderie that happens when you come upon people who are doing the same thing you are doing (e.g., running around a perfectly pleasant park with an old wash rag tied around your head and sweat sluicing down your back, trying not to look as though you're in pain). Joggers smile and wave at one another, and occasionally collapse side by side on the same bench. Cyclists ring their bells. Single fathers who are beginning to show the strain of conversing for six hours with their child and their child's imaginary friend, Coco, are usually delighted to meet a pretty and polite adult female who when introduced to Coco says, 'How very nice to meet you,

Coco. Haven't I seen you here before?' Dog-owners never tire of being complimented on their pets. 'Oh,' you say, as Little Brutus, tail wagging, comes up and sticks his nose in your crotch, 'What a friendly dog.' 'Isn't he?' beams Little Brutus' dad. You take a step backwards and Little Brutus takes a step forwards. You try giving his head a gentle nudge with your hand. If he were a cat, the sound he makes in response to this gesture might be mistaken for a purr. His breath is very hot. 'Is he always this friendly?' you grin. For the first time you notice that Little Brutus and his dad are wearing identical collars.

And, unlike trying to strike up a conversation with someone in the confines of the second act of *King Lear*, an afternoon in the park is fairly rife with opportunities. You can lend him a tissue to wipe the ice cream off his little girl's face or the dog shit from her shoes. You can throw the stick back. You can be hit by his bike. You can jog a few steps beside him and then faint. No longer restricted to opening conversational gambits such as 'Excuse me but I think you're sitting on my shopping', you are free to approach likely strangers and comment on their shorts or their thigh muscles or the marvellous condition of their pit bull terrier's teeth. Just as dog-owners like to talk about dogs and fathers like to talk about their children, cyclists like to talk about their bikes and all the close-calls they've had, and runners like to talk about their Nike trainers. There are conversations waiting to happen.

'Of course,' says Jane, 'if you're not really into strenuous physical exercise you should be careful. Aside from the risks of sprains and strokes and that sort of thing, you don't want to meet the love of your life when you're smelling like the locker room after the game. I would advise, therefore, that if you aren't sure just how much running or cycling you can do to sweat just enough to look both authentic and appealing, you simply walk. It's best to have either a dog or a small child by your side.'

Why?

'Because they make you seem non-threatening and usually give you something to say to a stranger, or vice versa.'

But what if you don't own a dog or a child?

'Borrow one.'

But isn't that dishonest?

'No, Serena, it is not dishonest. Every day of the year millions of people walk dogs and children who don't belong to them without being classified as criminals.'

Okay, okay. But what if you meet someone fascinating and irresistible while you're standing up to your thighs in a fountain, retrieving the frisbee or hunting for the socks, and he asks you to dinner on Sunday? What if you start seeing one another on a regular basis? Isn't he going to think it's strange that the kid's moved out?

'You're harping, Serena, aren't you? You're going back to the time I first invited Robin Clooney over for supper, forgetting that he was going to expect to see your dog Elwood sleeping on my couch.'

It was a little much, Jane telling him Elwood had been killed by a milk float.

Poetry Readings, Art Gallery Openings, Book Launches, etc.
Jane claims that the above occasions are the natural settings for meetings with men of intellect, charisma, highly developed right lobes, and the kind of status that will make your girlfriends envious rather than sympathetic.

'Are you kidding?' hoots Jane. 'I've met more absolutely phenomenal men at poetry readings and launch parties than you've had frozen dinners. They're all over the place. The agents and the publishers are all suave and suited and are always offering you another glass of wine, and the artists and writers are all witty and scruffy, but in an artistic way, and are always asking you if you know where they can get another glass of wine. I've got two jobs and passed three Open University courses because of men I'd met at this sort of thing.'

But why would anyone assume that men who go around quoting T.S. Eliot in conversational lulls, or dropping the names of obscure German painters the way most of us drop hints, or telling Philip Roth and Stephen King anecdotes while the rest of the gathering stands around them in a circle, are going to be any smarter, any more fun to be with, or of any more sterling character than the guy who fixes your roof?

Let's face it, the only men you are likely to find at poetry readings are poets and the friends of poets, who, like the friends of psychopathic killers, are loyal and well-intentioned but often a little naive. (I did once meet a very nice and very interesting person at a poetry reading, but she was the ex-wife of the poet, who agreed with me totally in my opinion that poets, though sometimes decorative and colourful enough if, at a very large party, you stick one in each room, leave a lot to be desired when it comes to daily life.) And who hangs out at gallery openings, drinking the free wine and arguing about Andy Warhol, but artists and broody agents and collectors? Book launches? The author (drunk), the author's editor (drunker), the author's friends (barely able to remember why they're there or what the title of the author's book is), every famous or influential person the author and the editor know (all of them talking about themselves), and a few bored-looking reviewers, eating up the meagre snacks before anyone else can get near them and knocking back the drinks as though they know something about the end of the world that no one else does.

And while it can't be denied that no man voluntarily misses an opportunity to talk about himself (unless you have just asked him for a specific piece of information like 'How do you really feel about my winning the Peace Prize, Harry?' or 'Since when are you so interested in the *I Ching*?'), men involved in the Arts seldom realize that there might be something to talk about at all.

'Hey, wait a minute,' you say. 'These guys don't sound so bad to me. The trouble is, I get invited over to my friend's for dinner and once I was invited to a wine tasting at the local Augustus Barnett, but I never get invited to gallery openings or book launches or poetry readings. So what do I do?'

This is no problem, according to Jane. Poetry readings, for instance, are almost always advertised in the entertainment guides under What Else Is Going On? No one has ever been turned away from a poetry reading, which is why the rumour has begun to spread that the homeless of our cities belong to the intellectual élite. To be invited to special showings and launches, however, usually requires a friend in the trade. Though not necessarily.

Jane used to go to every major publishing party in town simply by being devious. 'Not devious,' says Jane. 'By using my brains.' The first thing she would do was find out when, let's say, the new Joseph Heller novel was going to be published. Then she would call up the publisher and say that she worked for *The Times* and had mislaid her invitation. 'It's at the Bongo Club, isn't it?' she'd say. 'Eight-thirty?' And the girl at the publisher's would say, 'Oh, no, it's in the crypt at St Jerome's at seven.' Then all she had to do was turn up and move quickly through the door.

'Well, I don't know,' you say. 'I think I'd feel a little funny crashing a party like that. Wouldn't everyone know that I didn't belong? What if someone started talking to me?'

If no one starts talking to you there's no point in going.

'Well, that's true, of course, but what if I don't really know that much about literature? What if someone asks me something frightfully intelligent about James Joyce?'

The trick, Jane maintains, is to never feel out of place. 'Just say to yourself, "I have as much right to be here as anybody else", take a deep breath, and chuck yourself through the door. Three-quarters of the people milling around talking about structuralism have no reason to be there either. And out of the forty or so people all huddled together near the bar, the only one who will know much about literature will be the bartender or the woman who hands out the cream cheese and caviar on soggy biscuits. No one ever asks anything intelligent about James Joyce.'

Airports
Bus and train stations, says Jane, are often depressing and (like poetry readings and public libraries) filled with the homeless. They also are known for their substandard toilet facilities. Airports, however, are pleasant and spacious and make you think you're in a shopping centre rather than a film noir B movie. (This only applies to major airports, of course. Small, secluded airports, especially within the borders of the Soviet Union, can make you feel like you're in an episode of *The Twilight Zone*.) Airports have restaurants, shops, bars and, sometimes, even television. You can easily spend a day or two there, chatting to all the interesting men whose flights have been delayed, before anyone starts wondering why you never leave. Bring a good book or the afghan you've been crocheting for the past five years, says Jane, so that a man who wants to meet you can simply sit next to you and say, 'Hey, I read that. It's really great' or 'What is that you're making? A horse blanket?' You can carry everything you need in your 'hand luggage': food, your personal stereo system, reading matter, toiletries, change of clothes, a pocket chess set, hairdryer, make-up, curlers, hairspray, mouthwash, toothbrush,

perfume ... The cleanliness and spaciousness of most airport facilities, and the fact that during certain seasons of the year some people spend their entire holiday waiting for a plane, means that you can use the airport toilets with a familiarity and for a range of functions that you would not normally contemplate in the ladies' at Macdonalds. In fact, according to Jane, so many women find a few days at the airport as relaxing and re-enervating as a week at the seaside that there are clubs springing up in California that offer tours to airports all over the world. 'Think of it,' says Jane. 'Two days at Athens airport, two days at Heathrow, three days at O'Hare, a week at Moscow. You get to see the world and meet a wide-range of men at the same time. What could beat it?'

I, however, raised by a long line of sceptical women, can't help thinking that a person worried about being gunned down by a terrorist might rather stay home.

Divorce Courts
'Why not?' asks Jane. 'You know there will be men there, and you know they won't be married. Or not for long at any rate.'

But Jane, I say, what about broken hearts and the death of the family and all those cowboy songs about empty gin glasses and jumping in the river?

'Get smart, Serena,' snaps Jane. 'This is the late twentieth century, not a nineteenth-century romantic novel. The trouble with you old-fashioned women is that you're too sentimental. By the time a couple gets to court, hearts are likely to be the last thing either of them have that's broken. And even if you did happen to share a cab with a man who's a little upset about the fact that his wife's fiancé was at the hearing with a bottle of champagne, what could he possibly need more at that moment than female compassion and understanding?'

But Jane, I say, that's playing all the old games,

that's getting someone on the rebound, that's – '

 ' – what makes the world go round,' finishes Jane.

Funerals

Funerals? Is there a new callousness abroad in the land?

'No, no, no,' says Jane. 'You've got the wrong end of the stick as usual, Serena. Not real funerals.'

Oh, well, that's a relief.

'Strangers' funerals.'

I feel as though I may have missed something.

Jane's idea is this. You read the obituary column. When you see an announcement of the funeral of, say, a wealthy businessman (who can, therefore, be assumed to have known other wealthy businessmen, some of them under eighty-five) you ring it with your red felt-tip, dust off the black velvet suit you bought in a sale five years ago, slap one of those black lace things over your head, and off you go. 'You just turn up at the graveside,' says Jane, 'and attach yourself to the back of the group. Don't cry, but look as though you're struggling to maintain your dignity though you're very dazed by grief.'

'I have a question,' I said.

'Fire away,' said Jane.

'What if someone comes up to you and asks you who you are?'

Jane sighed. 'You know,' she said, 'sometimes I think you're completely hopeless. The whole idea is that someone comes up and asks you who you are.' She laughed. 'Not the widow, of course. But some sleek, urbane and incredibly rich and influential man with grey at the temples and platinum jewellery who watches you from across the grave and is so struck by your beauty and your haunted grief that he offers you a ride home in his limo.'

'Yes, but, Jane,' I persisted, 'surely once I get into the limousine and he's reviving us both with mugs of

Glenmorange on the rocks he's going to want to know what my connection with the deceased was?'

'Mumble.'

'What?'

'Mumble. Mumble something he can't quite understand, but do it in a way that makes it sound very very personal, so that it would be impossible for him to ask you again without seeming rude. Then he'll think you were either a mistress or an illegitimate child. And as soon as you've mumbled, ask him something about himself and he'll probably never ask you another embarrassing question again.'

More Things to Do

Go Shopping

Hardware shops are not, as we have noted in passing, the only commercial enterprises where the astute woman might expect to find an interesting (or uninteresting) member of the opposite sex. I do know several people, including my grandmother, who have met men in bookshops. In my grandmother's case, they bumped into each other in the crime section and he said, '*Born Guilty*. I've read that, it's fantastic.' And she said, 'It's a present for my granddaughter. Are you married by any chance?'

Jane, who has made something of a hobby out of shopping, has had a great deal of success with this method. There was her short-lived but passionate affair with Al, the butcher, begun when she asked him for reassurance that the pig who used to own the loin of pork she was buying had died with dignity. There was the flirtation with the greengrocer who thought she stopped in every afternoon to get scraps for her rabbit. There was the fling with the man encountered in the autosupply shop who offered to drive her home

with her tyre, her fuel pump and her emergency lights.

Men's clothing stores have real potential. They are quiet, and unless there's been a sudden rush of weddings and promotions in the area, uncrowded. You can browse, says Jane. You can take your time. You can make the assistant show you every tie, handkerchief and garter in the shop, while you observe the comings and goings of several other customers. If you have a natural flair for daring and original fashion and are shameless and brazen, you can even try on a suit. ('Men love women in drag,' says Jane. 'As long, of course, as they aren't really that way.') Record shops, apparently, are also a strong contender. Nothing wins a man over as quickly as agreement. 'Wow,' you say, 'you like Dave Bromberg, too. I was beginning to think I was the only person in the world who'd ever heard of him' – thus establishing right from the start that, unlike the man whose wife divorced him for listening to Bob Dylan all the time, he has found a woman who appreciates his taste.

Take up a Sport
Long gone are the days when many people thought that exercise was sitting by an open window taking drugs. Now everyone's into pumping iron and playing squash until their hearts fail. You sit down next to someone at a dinner party and the first thing he says to you is not, 'My, I do like that colour blue. It's very becoming', but 'What's your sport?' You're sitting in the doctor's waiting room, as you have been for several hours, reading what people were doing to their hair two summers ago, when this burly sort of man, who would be extraordinarily handsome if his nose weren't broken, limps in and sits next to you. Every time he tries to turn a page in the *National Geographic* he's somehow managed to take from the coffee table he winces with pain. 'My God, you poor man,' you say to him, 'please, let me help. What happened to you? A car accident?' 'No,' he says, in what you assume can't be his normal voice, 'rugby.'

'Sports make sense,' says Jane. 'You can kill two birds with one terrific, sensible and healthy stone. You can get in shape and meet someone to be in shape for at one and the same time. We're talking about the more genteel sports here. Like tennis. Tennis attracts a good class of person, you get to wear those cute little skirts that show off your legs, and after the game you can sit at the bar and drink gin and tonic.'

Tennis also attracts tennis coaches. The only well-behaved, honest, unselfish, decent and completely charming tennis coach there has ever been in the entire history of the universe was Bill Cosby. And even he wasn't really a tennis coach, but a spy. Because of its very nature, tennis coaching appeals to

men who are just that little bit vain and fond of
showing off. They know that they look good in white
and that their smile shows up well against their tan.
They are in an occupation where retirement comes
well before sixty-five, so they have to hustle. They are
in an occupation where one of the few perks is an
abundance of women in cute little skirts, showing off
their good legs, so they have a tendency to flirt and to
use more muscles than the ones in their arms and legs.
Like many people in a position of power, they often
become enamoured of the sound of their own voice
and convinced of their own rightness in matters great
and small. Referees are no better.

'My favourite activities, sport-wise,' says Jane, 'are
watersports.'

Oh, watersports. Perhaps Jane's onto something
here. My friend Zena met her first husband, Van,
while drowning. He dragged her out of the water and
gave her mouth-to-mouth resuscitation. 'You can't
imagine what it was like,' Zena later reported. 'I
suddenly find myself awake and vomiting all over the
poolside, and then someone hands me a towel and I
look up and there is this Greek god type, all blond and
brown and muscled with this concerned look in his
eyes. I would have fallen in love with Lassie, so I didn't
stand a chance with him.'

'Drowning is not what I had in mind,' says Jane.
'Swimming. Or water-skiing. Or surfing. Or white
water rafting.'

White water rafting? I know that, as a leisure
activity, it attracts a lot of rugged, attractively
weather-beaten men, but I wouldn't think that it was
recommended for anyone who minds getting wet with
her clothes on. I would also have thought that, like
deep sea fishing and the ritualized slaughter of
defenceless animals (hunting), white water rafting is
most popular among men who are attracted to death
(either their own or someone else's), and by men who

are out to prove their manliness, and by men who can think of only three activities that they like to share with women. Think of Hemingway. Think of *The Deerhunter*.

'Oh, for heaven's sake, Serena, stop getting carried away.'

Keep in mind Martin Lightfoot.

'That's cheating.'

Martin Lightfoot was the half-Indian guide Jane met the summer she went canoeing on the Allagash. Martin was big, strong, handsome as an elk and wild as a bear. 'He was just like all those amazing men you see in American films,' was Jane's comment at the time. 'You know, built like a small mountain, flannel shirts and a woodsman beard. Quiet and shy, always polite, very good with a knife and a gun. We made love on hillsides, against trees, in the rapids themselves. We were like animals. It was wonderful.' What happened, then? Did Martin turn out to be one of those Vietnam vets who has to live in the woods by himself because the war made him crazy and he wants to kill everyone? No, Martin, like a lot of other people, missed the war. What happened was that Martin never left the woods – or not for long. He didn't mind tents, caves, or remote unheated cabins, but put him in a house with other houses as close as a mile or two away, or in the honeymoon suite of the Ramada Inn, and he became a completely different person. More than forty-eight hours away from the possibility of being killed by a black bear or drowned in white water and it was goodbye Mr sweet, patient, warm-hearted, environmentally sound Nice Guy, and hello to the spectre that haunted northern Maine. 'By the second morning,' said Jane, 'he was morose and sullen and complaining about everything. The food wasn't fresh. The food was too fresh. He had a massive fight with the waiter because the hotel restaurant didn't have any canned baked beans. The bed was too hard. The water was too soft. The indoor lighting hurt his eyes. There wasn't enough soap. This from a man who lived inside a dead moose for two days during a blizzard. He was a great lover when you were upside down at the bottom of a rubber raft, but brought indoors you began to realize that what seemed like hours when your naked bottom was bouncing on the remains of an old campsite was only a matter of seconds on a mattress and box spring. What also became apparent was that aside from now and then shouting out a direction – you know, faster honey, slower, baby, not so hard – or telling you how soft your skin was, Martin didn't have a lot to say to a woman. I hadn't noticed that when we were shooting the rapids or building campsites because I was so busy trying not to fall in or get bitten by anything and admiring how he was one with nature. And in that sort of setting his stories of old woods lore and legends were great. But in the Pilgrim's Grill, with candles on the table and a Martini in your hand, the third re-telling of the tale of the beaver that lost its front paw wasn't so glamorous. And then I met his mother and that settled everything.' She didn't like you? 'Of course she liked me. She loved me. She said Martin was just like his father. She said she still remembered the winter she had to chop down the banisters for firewood because she had three small children and Martin's father had gone off for a hunting weekend in November and didn't come back till the Fourth of July. She said that if I stayed with Martin I would never see a wine bar or an opera again. She said I'd find myself waking up in the middle of the night, feverish and delirious, thinking that I'd just heard a bus go by outside the cabin.'

Use Couriers

Whenever possible, says Jane, have things delivered to you by courier. You know the postman, after all; there's not much fun in having him bring your mail. 'I once met this really adorable Australian this way,' says

Jane. 'He had a little ponytail and a smile just like Tom Cruise's. Late at night we'd race through the city on his bike. It was exhilarating.' It was also dangerous. 'It was the sort of accident that could have happened to anyone.'

'But what if I'm not the sort of person who needs to have things biked to her?'

According to Jane, it doesn't matter if you need it or not. Nothing cheers up a dull afternoon more than having someone all in leather turn up on your doorstep and in a deep, husky voice say, 'Is Ms Wishbone in?'

'But no one ever sends me anything by courier,' you complain.

'For heaven's sake,' says Jane. 'Use your imagination. Send it yourself.'

Go to Parties and Other Celebrations

Parties are what people have when they can't think of anything else to do or they owe so many people an invitation to dinner that the only way they can fulfil their social obligations before the end of the millennium is to have everyone over at once. If you go to enough parties, sooner or later it begins to feel as though you are stuck in a time warp and are going to the same party over and over. 'Can it be true?!' you exclaim, looking up from the bowl of dry roasted peanuts. 'I can't shake the feeling that I've been to this party before – eaten these nuts and tiny cheese crackers, drunk this wine, danced in this hallway ...' You taste the guacamole, you sniff the olives, you run an eye over the records waiting to be played. You listen to the conversation of the couple to your left about cryonic suspension. 'I have been here before!' you say out loud, 'I'm sure of it!' You even know that if you go to the downstairs toilet there will be someone locked in there, crying. You know at exactly what point the couple in black leather will begin to dance,

and what the woman with the loud voice will say about it. You know exactly who is going to end the evening by being sick in the wastebasket. You can tell which of the host's friends is going to bring the lamp table down when, during an argument about rugby vs football, he suddenly passes out.

There is no magic about this. It doesn't prove that you have lived this life before, or that, in your next incarnation, you're likely to come back as the Dali Lama. The simple truth is that they are all the same party. From the first one you ever went to when you were a teenager where someone fell asleep in the front garden to the one you went to last week where an especially dexterous couple broke the bathroom sink, there has only ever been one.

'Your problem, Serena,' says Jane, 'is that you have

no real spirit of adventure. You only go to the parties of people you know. Ergo, you already know everyone who's going to be there and what the fight's likely to be about before you've even done your eyes. Unless the cop who comes to the door at three in the morning is especially dishy, you aren't likely to meet anyone at a party like that. Just as with funerals, you've got to go to the parties of strangers.'

But Jane, if they're strangers they're unlikely to invite me.

'Nonsense. If you're friendly to people at the office, they'll invite you to their parties. If you are always on the lookout, you'll be in the queue at the deli right behind two lovely guys who are buying a crate of beer and fifteen bags of tortilla chips. Where do you think they're going? Follow them. Sometimes I just walk through the better neighbourhoods at night, waiting to feel the pavement pulse and see the bright lights shining from an upstairs window. Then in I go.'

And doesn't anyone ever ask you who you are?

'Sure.'

And what do you say?

'What do you think I say? I say I'm Jane Fforbes-Smythe.'

And doesn't anybody ask you who you know?

'I say I came with a friend. Edsel. That's always a good name to use. Very few people know anyone called Edsel. So they say, "Oh, I don't know him," and the subject is dropped.'

But what about the hostess and host?

'What about them? The only time I've ever actually spoken to a hostess at a party she was under the kitchen table and asked me to get her a drink. We became quite chummy.'

Celebrations on the other hand, are functions that serve a purpose. They celebrate – weddings, bar mitzvahs, anniversaries, graduations, promotions, christenings, divorces, the completion on the house.

With the exception, perhaps, of my second wedding (at which there were four people, including the nuptial couple, and one of them had to go home to get his wallet), most celebrations are larger than most parties. There is a more varied guest list. People come from different cities and counties, even countries. At a wedding, for example, (where a surprisingly large number of people – though not the bride and groom – fall in love) it is possible for the host and hostess to know only a handful of the guests and thus spend most of the day nudging each other and whispering out of the sides of their mouths, 'Who's the fat lady in the lilac organza?' (Mrs Blake, Eliza's mother, solved this problem at the wedding of her fourth daughter by making the guests wear name tags: John Houseman, friend of the groom. Lucinda Tucker, best friend of the groom's mother. Peggy McGuiness, Marsha's friend at the office.) So your chances of meeting someone you don't know are pretty good. It was at the name tag wedding, in fact, that Eliza met Judson, cousin of the groom. They struck up a conversation at the buffet table, and wound up laying bets as to which of the bride's mother's friends would later be found in the ladies', wondering out loud if the bride might be pregnant. The main reason that it didn't, in the end, work out for Eliza and Jud is one of the pluses of these big family celebrations that is also one of its problems: people come from all over. You go to a wedding and instead of falling in love with the groom's ex-flatmate, who lives and works in the same town as you, you fall in love with the bride's cousin who came all the way from Antarctica just for this. And if they've stuck you at one of those numbered tables it can take the whole evening to get away from the old school friend from Kenya (who is handsome, charming, funny, and knows all the family gossip) and over to the other side of the room, where lurk the groom's current friends (most of whom are schlumps, but local ones).

Even Jane has her reservations about weddings. 'There are always so many married men at weddings who drink half a bottle of free whisky and then want you to do the Mexican hat dance or the watusi with them,' she complains.

So you wouldn't recommend them?

'Oh, no,' says Jane. 'Of course I recommend them. The potential's enormous. But, if possible, you should have a glance through the guest-list beforehand, so you can sort out the married men quickly. And never, but never, bring an escort with you, no matter how much the bride's mother moans and groans about upsetting the numbers. Bringing a date to a wedding is like bringing a packed lunch and a can of beer.'

Buy or Sell a Used Car

Of course, you are not really going to buy a car, nor are you really going to sell one. You are just going to pretend. When Jane decided to sell a car she borrowed her brother's Midget for a week. (He was in Thailand on holiday, or he would never have agreed to this. Not since the time she sold his flat. What a palaver! 'You'd have thought,' said Jane, 'that he would've been flattered that I had sought and found a man with tastes so similar to his. But, oh no, all he could think about was that silly Roman vase.') She then slapped an ad in the local paper and sat by the telephone, polishing her nails. Because of the way she had phrased the advertisement (excellent mechanical condition, body needs a little work) the only responses she had were from men. Five men interested in sports cars (therefore, probably without a family) and capable of bodywork.

'It seems like a lot of trouble to go to just to meet a man,' I said.

'Just?'

'To,' I corrected myself. 'A lot of trouble to go to to meet a man.'

'What trouble?' Jane wanted to know. 'You think

that was work? I met a woman on my course who rented a 1953 baby-pink Cadillac convertible and then pretended to sell it.'

'And what happened?'

'She met two rock guitarists, one keyboard man, and an advertising agency executive.'

'And then what happened?'

'Well, that was a little unfortunate. The man who rented her the Cadillac in the first place saw the ad and turned up thinking he was going to get a twin to his. There was an awful row. But guess what happened in the end?'

'I'm almost afraid to.'

'She and the guy who rented her the Caddy got together. They've got two kids and she's become his partner and is quite a force in the automotive world.'

So there.

Buy a Dog

The obvious advantage that dogs have over other pets (with the exception, I would venture, of big cats and chimpanzees) is that they have to go out all the time. This makes them an entry into a community of people who are like-minded to the extent that it doesn't bother them that they are always covered in hairs and smell like wet wool. As we have already touched on in the section about parks, having a dog with you means that you always have something to start a conversation with.

Jane says that one shouldn't forget that there are also distinct advantages to breeding and showing. The community is smaller, but more intense. Instantly, you are among people with whom you, presumably, share a major passion. People who speak the same language, think the same thoughts, worry the same worries. People whose life-focus is as one with yours. The long-haired Chihuahua. The Springer Spaniel. The West Highland White.

Jane did have an unfortunate experience, however, when she started breeding Pekinese. She picked Pekinese not because she found them charming and endearing (rather, she thought that theirs was the sort of face best confined to cheap horror films), but because she found the man in the pet store, who owned five hairy, bug-eyed little champions, pretty charming and endearing. But to get intimately involved with an animal on this level you must really like it. You must really care if its ear is an eighth of an inch too long or it's got the wrong coloured spot on its foot. You can't have any qualms about cutting things off, or entertain for even a second the thought that teaching an animal to walk around a small ring with military precision is a pretty pointless way to spend both its and your time. You must never call it a poor excuse for multi-cell life in front of other enthusiasts.

There is also the fact to consider that dog-owners do tend to look like their dogs. Next time you're out walking, cast an eye on the dog and human couples you pass. And then think to yourself, if I start showing Corgis, not only are people going to start noticing how short my legs are, but I'm going to find myself living with a man with over-sized, pointy ears. Jane and Edward came to the parting of the ways one evening when they were dining out in this little Hungarian restaurant they frequented. The lights were low. The violins were playing. The aroma of paprika hung in the air like incense. They held hands across the table. She gazed longingly into his eyes. 'It was so bizarre,' said Jane the next day. 'But I suddenly realized that I didn't know if I was gazing into Edward's big, dewy brown eyes or Ninkumpoo the Third's. For a moment there I really thought Edward had a moist, black nose that looked like a wet handbag.'

'But the best thing about pets,' says Jane, 'is that they need vets.' Animals get ill, or go into bad depressions, or require shots – all situations that necessitate taking them to the doctor.

Unlike a great many medical doctors, who often seem to dislike their patients and find them an annoyance, veterinarians usually like theirs. They are sympathetic to them. It is not true that a man who likes dogs and gerbils can't be all bad, but there's at least an eighty-five per cent chance that he isn't. Jane says that the only difficulty here is that it is hard to see your vet on a regular enough basis to have the opportunity of diverting his attention from the cat's bald patch long enough to make him think of asking you out. 'Once,' says Jane, 'I fell in love with this vet named Abe. Every time he said, "If you'll just hold Portia still for a second, Ms Fforbes-Smythe, I'll give her a little injection. It won't hurt her a bit", my heart turned to warm toffee. But I never got to see him, you know? And when I did get to see him he was looking into Portia's mouth or sticking a thermometer up her bum. It didn't matter what I wore or what I smelled like, he never noticed. I figured I had to do something drastic or the most intimate conversation we would ever have would be about defleaing Portia's bedding.'

'So what did Jane do?' you clamour.

What Jane did was borrow ill and injured animals. One a month. In October it was her mother's spaniel, in November it was a friend's tabby cat, in December it was the hamster of the little girl next door. She reached Buckwheat (who is not a happy traveller, nor a very well-behaved patient) in April.

'Well,' you say excitedly, remembering the dashing vet who showed you how easy it is to spray a cat the last time you took yours in for a visit, 'did it work?'

Not exactly. It worked in the sense that he began calling her by her name instead of her cat's name. 'Well, hey there, Jane,' he'd say, 'and what can we do for you today?' But it didn't work in the sense that he started dating the owner of an iguana.

Eat Breakfast

Clearly, if you're eating breakfast at your own kitchen table, like most normal people, with the cat on your lap and the toast burning gently in the grill, you are not going to meet anyone unless someone breaks in. You have to go out.

'Go out? For breakfast?'

Business people, apparently, do it all the time. So do bachelors and commuters who had no time for more than a cup of coffee before they rushed from the house.

'What's great about going out for breakfast,' says Jane, 'is that it's so subtle. Who's expecting to be seduced over his bacon and eggs? Besides Warren Beatty, Serena.'

For this reason, Jane maintains, meeting men at breakfast is a relaxed and pleasant way to spend a half hour or so. There's no pressure, no expectations, you can be yourself. Your make-up is fresh and your suit hasn't yet started to wrinkle. If you are a morning person, you are radiating health and energy and a glorious disposition. If you are a night person you are still at home in bed.

'Pick somewhere in the centre of the city,' says Jane, 'somewhere where there are lots of businesses and offices. This gives you scope. Hotel restaurants are also good, of course, but there again you run the risk of striking up a promising friendship with some guy who is only sixteen hours away from Budapest.'

So, okay, here you are on a bright Friday morning, shoes polished, wearing your favourite dress and carrying a fashionable attaché case, gliding through the doors of the Cup and Saucer. You look around. There are a few seats at the counter, but the tables are all taken. You give the taken tables a quick once-over. At a table against the wall, reading a newspaper that has more words than pictures, is a nice looking man in the sort of suit that suggests that he has a good job but doesn't work in a bank. You can't see a wedding ring. You wish that Sherlock Holmes were with you so he could tell you a little more about this guy, but failing that you stroll over to his table and say, 'I'm sorry to disturb you, but I was wondering if I might share your table, I do so hate sitting on those wooden stools.' He will, of course, say, yes. He's a gentleman. He's almost finished. You're not crying or anything. In fact, you look pretty nice yourself. 'Sure,' he says, 'be my guest.' You make sure you order eggs so that you have to ask him to pass the salt.

'Don't just confine this technique to breakfast, though,' says Jane. 'A woman should have no inhibitions about eating any meal – lunch, supper, brunch, an after-theatre snack – out on her own, but she should have even less about approaching an interesting man and asking to share his table. Always go to very popular and crowded restaurants, of course, or it might look a little obvious.'

Join Something

When you were a kid and used to mope around the house during school holidays, complaining that your brain was dying of boredom and there was nothing to do, your mother used to tell you to join a group. 'Why don't you join a theatre group?' she'd ask. 'Why don't you go to the Bible classes?' 'Why don't you volunteer at the hospital?' And you always said no. You always made a disgusted face and sighed and groaned and informed her once more that she didn't understand anything. Now Jane is giving you this same advice.

It doesn't really matter what you join. The church discussion group. The neighbourhood writing circle. Alcoholics Anonymous. A birdwatcher's club. A string quartet. Anything that will get you out of the house and into the vicinity of some eligible men.

'Alcoholics Anonymous is one of the best groups to join,' says Jane 'because you are almost guaranteed that the men there have lost their wives and sweethearts long ago, when they used to get drunk every night and throw the television through the living room window. And now that they're sober, and the really nice guys they always were deep down, they need a woman by their side to love and support them. They're looking. But all the women they know remember when they couldn't speak after four in the afternoon. They remember going out for dinner with them and ending up going home alone because their escort passed out with his face on the table. They remember the time he simply started sliding down the wall in the middle of a conversation about favourite things. And that's where you come in.'

Yeah, but Jane, surely Alcoholics Anonymous doesn't encourage people who don't have a drinking problem in their life to just come in off the street and eat the brownies.

'Oh, Serena,' sighs Jane, 'you just don't ever learn.'

Go on Holiday
The trouble with our real lives is that it gets into routines, it becomes stratified. Here you are, beautiful, vivacious, intelligent, scintillating, energetic, kind, compassionate, funny, original, loving, an expert on rock-and-roll, pre-war crime novels and *chilis rellenos* – but who knows? Who appreciates you? The men you tend to see in the course of a normal day all think of you in specific ways. There's Ms Wishbone, the woman who buys the low-fat milk. There's Ms Wishbone, the woman who never has the right change for the bus. There's Ms Wishbone, the woman who always floods the launderette. There's Ms Wishbone, the woman who's always pushing her Volkswagen. There's Ms Wishbone, whose desk is so neat everyone always assumes she's away for a week. They don't look at you and see a woman who can fandango for five hours straight with a rose between her teeth. They

look at you and see a woman who's going to give them a hard time about the avocados. They don't see you walk by on your way to the coffee machine and think, wow, I sure would like to share a plate of nachos with her. They think, oh brother, if I don't get that report done by Wednesday she's going to do me some bodily harm. How can a man who only sees you when you're weeping because the car stalled in traffic again be expected to easily imagine you laughing in the middle of a nude pillow fight?

The solution is to get away from your real life every so often and enter the never-never land where no one has to get up for work in the morning or do the dishes or meet deadlines or keep appointments or fulfil any obligations other than paying the bar bill from time to time. The solution is to go somewhere where no one has any preconceived notions of you; where every man you meet is going to be asking himself whether you're unattached and interested days before he asks himself whether or not you're a stickler for details. The solution is to go on holiday.

'By myself?'

'Not necessarily,' says Jane. 'You can take a trusted girlfriend along. But keep in mind that female bonding often breaks down when there are men around. It's nothing we intend, it just happens. It's because of the way we've been brought up. If you're both interested in the same man, you could be facing two weeks of silence and thudding bathroom doors in a 12' × 4' bungalow in Greece. Two weeks of polite and well-mannered requests for a little less noise, or a little more light, or the whereabouts of the suntan lotion. Two weeks of finding that whenever you leave your swimsuit at the bottom of the bath tub someone else has pointedly hung it out to dry. The situation is no better if the friend you go away with is a bit more on the stunningly beautiful side than you are. Then you wind up being the person who writes out all the postcards, and goes shopping for all the souvenirs, and eats all the hotel meals – hers and yours – because they're included and you can't stand to see them go to waste. You become the person she and the young god she's fallen in love with feel sorry for. Poor Ms Wishbone. "Why don't you come on the paddle boats with us?" she asks, genuinely concerned that you're spending too much time in the hotel bar, writing postcards. And you reply, "Oh, no, you know how sensitive my skin is" – and not the truth, which is that you might try to drown her.

'So if you want to go with a friend, which is, of course, a great thing to do, Serena, I agree with you completely, make sure that you make a non-competition pact beforehand. I, however, usually prefer to go alone.'

Many women cannot imagine going on holiday by themselves. What they can imagine is themselves sitting on the beach, cream on the nose and Raybans on the eyes and a 400-page paperback on the stomach, surrounded by canoodling couples or young families that look as though they just stepped off the cover of a Thompsons' brochure – and then they can imagine themselves drinking a bottle of gin to get through the rest of the day. They can picture themselves eating all by themselves at a table for one whose candle no one ever bothers lighting, putting on a brave face over the roll and coffee but eventually snivelling into the moussaka at the end of the day. They can see themselves sitting on a chair in the corner at the disco, smiling grimly at the happy holidayers, finally agreeing to dance with the waiters.

In reality, few things are more enjoyable than the single holiday. You learn to rely on yourself in unusual situations. You learn to utilize your inner resources. You don't stay safely by the pool for two weeks because the person you came with has sunstroke or headaches or doesn't like looking at old buildings. You

discover your own yearning for adventure, disguised
for years by an inordinate fear of having to
impersonate a chicken in order to get anything to eat.
You discover that you are, in fact, a very sociable
person who makes friends easily but who also enjoys
being on her own.

'You discover,' says Jane, 'that there are quite a few
unattached and not unattractive men around who are
looking for someone to blow in their ear under the
romantic August moon while the stars twinkle and the
hotel band plays "I Want to Hold Your Hand".'

For on holiday you can be who you will. None of the
men that you meet, from the tour guide to the hotel
manager to the man in 283 who keeps to himself and is
reputed to be here 'on business', have any ideas about
you. You are exciting and mysterious. You are sensual
and sophisticated. You can wear fire-engine red
lipstick and sprinkle your shoulders with flecks of
glitter. You can let your hair down, flirt and be
outrageous, and no one's going to tell your mother. No
one's going to come up to you in the corridor in
December and say 'Hey hey hey, remember the way
you were dancing with that guy with the eye patch in
that empty swimming pool last summer?'

Hang Around Outside of the Gents'
Oh, hey, Jane, not every gents' toilet is well suited for
this activity, you know. You wouldn't want to hover
too long outside the toilets of most bus and train
stations or subways, where the chances of being
gunned down by a terrorist would be the least of your
worries. 'Of course not,' agrees Jane. 'But if you do a
little lingering outside the toilets of the better hotels
and restaurants you may be surprised to discover just
how many interesting-looking men use public toilets
for the purposes for which they were originally
intended.'

The trick, says the expert, is not to look as though

you are loitering, but as though you are either waiting for your girlfriend to come out of the ladies' or trying to get the cigarette machine to work.

'Okay,' you say, 'so I'm standing there, humming some simple show tune and looking expectantly towards the ladies' every so often, and this really great looking man comes out and gives me the same sort of look that I'm giving him. Then what do I do?'

You do the equivalent of what your great-grandmother would have done (which is drop her lace-edged, lilac-scented hankie). You drop your handbag. Of course, you must make sure that your handbag is open and going to spill out all over as it falls. There is little as efficient as crawling under a cigarette machine at the Hilton to retrieve a stranger's tube of mascara for breaking the ice. Before the last foreign coin and plastic stirrer have been returned to your bag he will be suggesting a drink at the bar.

'And in some cases,' continues Jane, 'you may want to abandon your post in the foyer and actually walk into the gents' by mistake. "Oh, my goodness!" you exclaim, your eyes on the eyes of the dashing, magnetic man who prompted you to abandon all your mother's teachings. "Wrong room." He probably won't say anything for a few seconds. Into that silence you say, "Hey, has anybody ever told you how much you look like Bruce Springsteen!" '

Get Arrested
You think it's a little extreme, don't you?

'No such thing,' says Jane. 'I mean, it's not as though you have to go out and rob a bank or cosh somebody over the head or anything. You don't even really have to get arrested, you just have to have a reason for making the acquaintance of some officers of the law. The advantage in being arrested, however, is that you're not restricted to only policemen, if you know what I mean.'

Jane is thinking of the time Jenny was arrested for dodging her fare on the bus. Malcolm was being booked for kicking a laundry basket down the street and thus obstructing traffic (it's one of those long stories). After they were released they went for a drink together to commiserate. By the end of the evening they were talking about the strange coincidences of life and how it sometimes seems as though there must be a plan. Destiny was mentioned more than once. 'I mean,' Jenny said to me the next day, 'how would I ever have met him if this hadn't happened? He's a marine biologist and I teach in a primary school. He lives in a large body of water and I live in a small inland flat. He'd never kicked a laundry basket down the street before and I'd never lost my bus ticket. Kismet.'

And then, of course, there was also the time Jane was arrested.

'It was a small arrest, and mainly a misunderstanding. I'd rather talk about the time I was burgled and the officer who came to take the report invited me out for dinner.'

I'd rather talk about the time you were arrested and the officer who caught you invited you out for dinner.

'But that's the whole point, Serena, policemen are always asking out the attractive, respectable women they meet in the course of their work. If they didn't, it'd be like working in a restaurant and never having a sandwich or a bit of pudding.'

What an attractive way of putting it.

11

THE HOW CAN YOU TELL IF HE WON'T COMMIT, WANTS YOU TO LOVE HIM TOO MUCH, REALLY HATES WOMEN, OR REALLY LOVES YOU SO? QUIZ

Okay, you've followed Jane's faultless advice and approached the problem in a straightforward, scientific, twentieth-century manner. No slopping sentimentality. No shyness and behaviour hang-ups. No waiting for him to find you. You've shambled through hundreds of food stores, got to know every hardware emporium and lumber yard within a twenty-mile radius, were three days late with the annual report because of the darts tournament, and have bought every male you know Christmas and birthday presents for the next eight years. And it worked. You found someone. The question now is, exactly who is it you've found? Is he going to turn out to be one of life's great non-committers? Or is he really the Coca-Cola of your heart? Select the most appropriate answer honestly. No cheating. No giving him the benefit of the doubt. If he doesn't call for four days after promising he would ring you 'tomorrow' you cannot decide that this is because his phone was broken when he went to call, he rushed into the street to use the pay phone with only his phone card in his pocket, he was involved in a freak accident between a motorcycle messenger, a cheese van and a telephone box and now lies in coma in hospital, murmuring your name. You cannot give him extra points because though he was four hours late for your dinner party and turned up smelling of Jack Daniels and with no coherent excuse, you really understand him and know that he was only late because he was afraid of meeting your boss. Don't say to yourself, 'Ezekiel may be my last chance to have someone else to cook and clean and wash for; I don't want to put myself in a position where I might lose him,' and then put down that he gave you a present for your birthday when all it was was two tickets to a sumo wrestling match that he wanted to see.

1. It was lust and longing at first sight. You were trapped in one corner of the Crabshaws' party with

your back against a wooden duck decoy while a very sweet woman who reminded you slightly of your father's sister before she started covering everything in the house in brown paper, told you about her past lives. Just as you were beginning to think that your present life was taking as long as her fourteen previous ones put together, you saw this slight but imposing figure over by the drinks table, finishing off the miniature quiches. Interrupting a rather colourful if complicated story of life in China in the first century, you made your excuses and hot-footed it over to this hungry man. You asked him to pass you a cheese football. Your eyes met. A tiny flake of pastry floated down from his moustache to his floral tie. 'Do you come here often?' he quipped. Since then, though as you are both rational and mature people who have weathered several heavy relationships no one has spoken of 'love' or even 'deep liking', you and Albie have seen each other at least four nights out of every seven, and you have a toothbrush that has permanent residence in his bathroom. One morning as you're getting dressed, you say, 'Albie, honey, we've been seeing each other for more than six months now and, frankly, I'm getting a little tired of having to carry a suitcase around with me all the time so that I have a change of clothes for the morning. I know that people on the train must think I'm a call girl, and all my friends at work call it 'love luggage'. Don't you think I could have a drawer in your dresser – just to leave a few things?' He

a. says, 'Of course, Ms Wishbone. I was going to suggest it myself, as a matter of fact, but I didn't want you to think that I was pushing you or making demands. You'll find the middle drawer is free. What can we do to celebrate?
b. doesn't say anything for a second or two, and

then he puts on a fiendish little voice and cackles, 'Ohhoho, I should have known this would happen, my sweet. First it's the toothbrush, then it's a drawer in the dresser – you women are crafty creatures, mark my words, hehehehe.' He rolls his eyes back in his head so that only the whites are showing, and does something peculiar with his teeth. 'But who can blame you,' he continues, 'when I'm so irresistible.' You take this as a maybe.

c. sighs, takes another look in the mirror, and starts undoing his tie, an expression on his handsome face that suggests that his having to redo his tie is your fault. 'I knew this was coming,' he says at last. 'It never fails. You meet a woman you like, you have a nice time with her, and right away she starts edging in, making plans, taking over. All of a sudden everything is 'we' and 'us'. Next thing you know you'll be helping me pick out my clothes and telling me where I'm going on my holiday.' He throws the tie on the floor in disgust and bangs out of the room. That night he calls you and asks if you want to go to a film. Just before the lights go down, he says, 'Oh, by the way, Ms Wishbone, in case you're wondering what happened to it, I put that pair of socks you left behind this morning in the middle drawer of my dresser. There was a little extra room.'

2. You and Richard have been seeing each other since the summer. You met at a friend's barbecue. Richard was holding the umbrella over the grill and you were protecting the condiments with a raincoat. He impressed you immediately with his unflappability and coolness. He is several years older than you, and that combined with the way he instantly took control when the hamburgers started getting wet was enough to convince you of his maturity and sensibility. Now it is nearly Christmas. You and Richard have been spending quite a bit of

time together. He has introduced you to his children by his first two wives. He let you bake the cake for his birthday party. He has given you a lot of advice on your relationship with your mother. You have sort of assumed, therefore, that you and Richard would be spending Christmas day together, and so you have turned down all other invitations. A week or so before the day itself you say, 'So, what shall I make for our Christmas dinner?' He

a. looks up from the book he is reading, looking slightly bemused. 'Well actually love,' he says, 'I thought that since you made the cake and the spicy tofu dip for my birthday party it was my turn. I was going to make us a quiet dinner for two, and I thought that in the evening we might ask my kids over for drinks.'

b. slaps his forehead (an expressive gesture considering the fact that he is driving at the time) and says, 'Oh my gosh, how will you ever forgive me? I'm terribly sorry, Ms Wishbone, but I had so many people after me for Christmas dinner that I finally gave up in despair and invited them round to me.' You turn to wipe steam off the window on your side and to keep him from seeing your trembling lower lip. 'Of course,' he continues, that little devilish grin that you like so much playing around his mouth, 'I was rather hoping you might come, too. I'm not quite sure I'm up to making gravy.' Both your laughter tinkles like sleigh bells in the car.

c. keeps his back to you as he locks the door. 'Christmas dinner? For us?' he asks. 'But Ms Wishbone, I have six children, four of them over the age of twenty. Don't you think some if not all of them might want to spend the holiday with me?' You feel humbled. In the end it turns out that none of them do want to spend the holiday with him, so you cancel the last-minute sympathy invitation you were given and roast an unhappy chicken (the butcher was all out of free-range turkeys by the time you got there).

3. You and Larry are at a party being held by his very best friend, and all the people who have known Larry for years (as compared to the weeks you have known him) are there. For this occasion (just the thought of which makes your palms sweat) you have spent two weeks' pay on this absolutely incredibly stupendous dress and shoes that make your feet look as though they touch the ground a good six inches before they actually do. You've had a massage, a sauna, a facial, an hour on the sunbed, and highlights put in your otherwise mousy hair. You've met a few people, chatted pleasantly about this and that, and are beginning to think that it isn't going to be so bad after all when the door opens and this good-looking woman, understated but elegant in a silk shirt and faded jeans, walks in. There is an audible hush in the room, and all eyes move from her to Larry. Her eyes find Larry's so quickly that for a second you think you might be in a play. People begin to talk again, suddenly and loudly, and the woman at the door starts slowly across the room. Larry

a. says 'That, in case you were in any doubt, is Barbara.' He puts his arm around you and gives you that little smirk he gives you when he knows you're the only other person in the room who will get the joke. 'Come on,' he says, 'I want her to meet you.' You immediately realize that you could have worn old jeans, too, and saved yourself a fortune.
b. winds one arm around your shoulder, much as though you and he are both members of the same

football team, and says, 'Do my eyes deceive me, or is that really Barbara the bitch?' He continues, 'You see before you one of the great ballbusters of contemporary Western civilization. A woman who makes Cleopatra look like a Girl Guide leader.' He pats you on the shoulder. 'You wait here, my girl,' he says jovially. 'I don't want you exposed to bad influences. I'll be right back.' It is later, when you're helping the hostess clear up, that you find him passed out on the floor of the bedroom where the coats were put.

c. starts smiling as though he doesn't know who just farted. When Barbara more or less floats to a stop in front of him, he says, 'You look wonderful,' and gives her a self-conscious peck on the cheek. They exchange a rush of words as people who are overly excited about seeing each other after a long time will, and then, in the middle of telling her a joke, his hand accidentally hits you and he says, 'Oh my goodness, how rude of me. Barbara, let me introduce ... Mela ... Suza ... B ... ' 'Ms Wishbone,' you offer, in a voice halfway between homicide and tears. Barbara says, 'How nice to meet you,' and that is the last word either of them address to you for several hours. Eventually you wander off on your own. Then you go home. At two in the morning you are woken up by Larry, drunk and overwrought, who spends the next six hours telling you all about how Barbara broke his heart.

4. On one of those intimate nights when the fire crackles and the snow stampedes against the window and you can't remember ever before feeling so happy, so contented, so at peace, you decide to tell the man on whose chest you rest your head about Lionel, at one time the great love of your life, a man on whom you wasted (including aftermath, period of mourning and convalescence)

nearly a decade, because Lionel was one of the most important happenings in your life and you think it is important that he is not kept secret. He

a. listens quietly to every damp detail, commenting only when he has something to say, gets up more than once to make coffee or get another drink, and in the end, as dawn tentatively fights its way through the ongoing storm, says, 'I'm really glad you trusted me enough to tell me about that, Ms Wishbone, you're a person I can really feel close to.'

b. listens quietly for awhile (but with an expression on his face that might mean that he's wondering whether or not he should have got a second estimate on the repairs to his car), and then, when emotion makes you pause before going on to the most painful part of the story, starts telling you about how devastated he was when Desiree, his great love, decided to follow her husband to Hong Kong after all.

c. says, 'Look, Ms Wishbone, I'm no more interested in hearing about your old boyfriends than I am in hearing the details of your last visit to the gynaecologist.'

5. For months he's been talking about showing you the part of the country he comes from. Every time he sees a car ad on the television or catches a glimpse of a sunset or has mashed potatoes for lunch he says to you, 'Oh, Ms Wishbone, if only I could show you Lower Sodding. There isn't a more beautiful place on the face of the earth. If you see it you'll know the real me.' One night when you are curled up against him, getting to know the unreal him, you say, 'Look, we've both got holiday time coming up. Let's go to Lower Sodding. I can't think of anywhere I'd rather see.' He says,

a. 'This is wonderful. I'll call my family first thing in the morning. When do you think you'd like to leave?'

b. 'This isn't really the right time of year.'

c. 'Ms Wishbone, there are several other people who want to go with me. I'll have to let you know.'

6. It is a glorious Saturday morning. The sky is blue, the grass is green, and the sun is shining its heart out. You and your amor had a wonderful night together, and this morning he is calling you his little Carebear, and you are calling him Sweet Hot Papa. In this mood, you offer to make breakfast. He sits at the table, squeezing the oranges for juice, while you prepare the eggs. You put the eggs in the saucepan. What happens next?

a. He finishes fixing the juice, gets up to throw the peel away, and gives you a little hug in passing. 'I'll do the toast,' he says, 'while you fry the bacon.' During breakfast he dips his little soldiers in your egg and you dip yours in his. After breakfast you go back to bed.

b. He is having such a hard time with the oranges that he doesn't notice that you don't know how to boil an egg. 'I've never even seen this done before,' he grumbles, his afterglow already long gone. 'Why don't you get a juicer like I've got?' Pips are flying everywhere, there is juice all over his hands and on the table, and a litle bit of orange innard has attached itself to his left eyebrow. 'I don't want a juicer,' you say. 'I'm happy with the old-fashioned method.' 'But it's so primitive, Ms Wishbone,' he grunts. 'Are you some sort of reverse snob?'

c. 'Darling,' he says, looking up from his task. 'What on earth are you doing?' 'Sweetie Pie,' you say, 'I'm boiling eggs.' 'Like that?' he asks, his voice not quite as warm as it was last night when he asked you if his hands were cold. 'Yes,' you say, a smile still playing on your rosebud lips, 'like this.' 'That's not the way you boil eggs,' he says, now using exactly the tone he uses when you do the driving. 'It's the way I boil eggs,' you explain, your smile gone grim. 'Darling,' he says, 'you're doing it wrong.' There then ensues a forty-five-minute debate on the right and wrong method of boiling an egg. You go through every cookbook on your shelf and find that of the two that actually address themselves to the issue, one favours putting the eggs in before you boil the water and one after. He says the first book is wrong, too. Although you find it hard to believe that you have become a person who argues about something as petty as this, you call your mother. You tell your mother what the problem is. 'Well,' says your mother, 'I used to boil eggs the way you do, but your father made me stop.'

7. When you first started seeing Aloyisious, he was very clear about laying out the ground rules of your relationship. He can't stand jealousy and possessiveness. You, who have too much self-esteem and inner security to be either jealous or possessive, agreed. He calls you one night when you said you'd be home, painting the bathroom, but there is no answer. How does he handle this?

a. The next time he sees you he says, 'I called you the other night to remind you that *Bedtime for Bonzo* was on. Did you remember to set your video?'
b. When you get home at nine o'clock he is sitting outside your flat, a bucket of fried chicken and a six-pack of beer beside him. 'I missed you,' he says. 'I thought I'd come over and give you a hand.'
c. He is on your doorstep at eight in the morning,

just passing on his way to work. 'Would you like some coffee?' you say, surprised to see him. He keeps peering over your shoulder and sniffing the air. 'What I would like,' he says, 'is an explanation.'

8. Archibald likes to think of himself as something of a sexual innovator. The Alexander Graham Bell of the bedroom, as it were (although, of course, a bedroom isn't always necessary). One night you decide to surprise Archibald with something you learned in Walthamstow. He

  a. says he'd be happy to die in your arms.
  b. loses his erection.
  c. is in, out, and sound asleep before you've moved into the second position.

So what (or who) have you got? Score one (1) point for every a. Two points (2) for every b. And three points (3) for every c.

If your man scores eight points exactly, he is definitely Coca-Cola. He is, in fact, so well-balanced, rational, reasonable, sensitive, intelligent, good-humoured and mature that it is almost difficult to believe he is human, let alone male. Are you sure you've been totally honest?

If your man scores between eight and thirteen he is not afraid to commit, he doesn't want you to love him too much, he has nothing against women, and he is probably pretty fond of you. He has the occasional grey area in his personality and psyche, but on the whole he is trying for perfection and his little flaws are almost endearing. It is anybody's guess why he has remained single long enough for you to meet him, but there are some bonuses in this world that defy any simple explanation, and he is clearly one of them.

If your man scores between thirteen and sixteen he, like cheap cake, looks better than he may actually be.

Underneath his reasonable surface lurks the tiny little heart of a man who wants you to do a lot more committing than he thinks he should have to do. It wouldn't bother him a great deal if you loved him too much, that's for certain. He has moments of sensitivity and caring when his defensiveness and insecurity are cast aside, but it is these moments when he is at his most endearing, not the moments when a little human frailty peeks through. The human frailty he's got down pretty patly.

Between sixteen and twenty-one denotes a man with some serious problems. There are less moments of sensitivity and caring and more moments of mistakenly thinking that the population of the planet is limited to himself. If you've got a man who scored twenty-four, however, there is no difficulty in understanding why he's still available. What is difficult to understand is why he has managed to live so long without being shot.